Solutions to Women's Hair Thinning & Loss

Solutions to Women's Hair Thinning & Loss

JEFFREY PAUL

THOMSON

DELMAR LEARNING

Australia   Canada   Mexico   Singapore   Spain   United Kingdom   United States

Solutions to Women's Hair Thinning & Loss
Jeffrey Paul

President, Milady:
Dawn Gerrain

Director of Editorial:
Sherry Gomoll

Editorial Assistant:
Jessica Burns

Director of Production:
Wendy A. Troeger

Production Coordinator:
Nina Tucciarelli

Composition:
Stratford Pub Services

Cover Design:
Joseph Villanova

Director of Marketing:
Wendy Mapstone

Channel Manager:
Sandra Bruce

Marketing Coordinator
Kasmira Koniszewski

Library of Congress Cataloging-in-Publication Data:

Paul, Jeffrey (Jeffrey Paul Mroczka)
    Solutions to women's hair thinning and loss / Jeffrey Paul.
      p. cm.
    Summary: "Presents information for hair-care professionals on the causes and treatment of hair thinning and loss in women. Includes step-by-step procedures for treating hair loss"— Provided by publisher.
    Includes index.
    ISBN 1-4018-4080-9
    1. Baldness—Prevention. 2. Hair—Care and hygiene. 3. Women—Health and hygiene. I. Title.
RL155.P38 2005
616.5'46—dc22   2004023331

NOTICE TO THE READER

CONTENTS

Contents

FOREWORD

For over forty-five years I have enjoyed being a part of the beauty industry, as a salon owner, co-founder of Matrix Essentials, and now as chairman of the board of Salon Quest, creators of Aquage Hair Products. My dream has always been to enhance the image and professionalism of salon owners and hair stylists. As professionals we have a license to touch our clients' lives and build special relationships with them, as we make them look better and feel better. We are in a beautiful industry.

Hair has long been called a woman's "crowning glory." Few things are as devastating to a woman's self-image as severe hair loss. The problem has grown more widespread in recent years for reasons that include heredity, illness, hormonal changes, medications, and physical and emotional stress. In fact, 25 percent of all women in the United States will experience some hair thinning (at best), and baldness (at worst) during the course of their lives. When a woman comes to the realization that she needs professional help to combat severe hair loss, she will first turn to her trusted stylist for help, support, and direction. *Solutions to Women's Hair Thinning & Loss* will help you to guide her through this difficult time.

Jeffrey Paul is the owner of Restoring Beautiful Hair. During his 30-plus successful years as a stylist, consultant, speaker, and hair replacement expert, he has continually expanded his outreach to help his clients experience both their inner and outer beauty. Paul and his wife, Zina, are the compassionate and energetic founders of Wigs for Kids, an organization with which I am proud to be affiliated. Wigs for Kids provides free high-quality human-hair wigs for children who have lost their hair because of medical reasons.

Paul collaborated with some of the best stylists and hair replacement specialists in the world while writing this comprehensive book. As a result, he offers excellent solutions and resources for salon professionals to meet their clients' needs. While this book provides solutions to a variety of specific hair-loss problems, it also teaches beauty professionals how to help their clients go beyond a skin-deep realization of their situation and discover their inner beauty.

This book blends spiritual, emotional, psychological, and practical advice from both personal and professional perspectives. Paul's caring and compassionate approach, along with his incomparable knowledge of every aspect of hair styling and replacement, will inspire salon owners and beauty professionals who work with women experiencing the loss of both their hair and self-esteem, and guide them to make these women's lives beautiful.

—SYDELL L. MILLER
FOUNDER OF MATRIX ESSENTIALS

IT'S ONLY HAIR—
Or Is It?

HAIR: The Crowning Glory and the Mission

Since practically the beginning of time, women have looked for ways to improve their looks and sustain their natural-born beauty. Yet, especially in today's times, when women have more internal and external stresses to deal with than ever before, more women face the problem of losing their luscious locks and are presented with precious few facts on the subject or potential solutions to the problem.

Hair is to a woman as the summit is to its mountain. It is very much the defining peak—something of awe even—to that which supports it. Without it, or with the deterioration of it, the glory of what remains seems to be diminished, and this awe-inspiring mountain inwardly and outwardly withers.

In a similar way, a woman's hair is not attached only to follicles in her scalp. It is also attached to her emotions, her sexuality, her personality, and her confidence—the way she feels about herself and, as a result, the way she interacts with the world. The anxiety that accompanies the first signs of hair thinning can shift to panic as she sees her familiar appearance becoming compromised.

Hair loss can be devastating to a woman. Some chemotherapy patients have said that losing their hair was so horrible its impact surpassed that of the disease for which they were being treated in the first place. For these women, regaining a comforting sense of their own appearance was an essential step in their healing process.

While such examples are extreme, they are not unusual. Whether the hair loss is mild, moderate, or severe, invariably it has a detrimental effect on a woman's sense of self that can affect every aspect of her life. As any woman who has ever struggled with hair loss can testify, hair is not just hair. Restoring a woman's beautiful hair again—or giving her a head of hair that is more beautiful than she ever dreamed she could have—is a powerful way to enable her own inner beauty to shine forth. With the understanding of how imperative healthy and beautiful hair can be to each individual, let's consider the state of affairs in the United States today that shows how much opportunity you have to help people with your skills and your business.

America's baby boomers are aging—and they're losing their hair. Of this huge cohort—81 million strong—about 30 million boomers are facing hair thinning and hair loss. And every day, more of the boomers who are losing their hair are women. Among American women aged 40 to 49, as many as 36 percent are worried about some degree of hair thinning or loss. Among American women of all ages, 25 to 30 million are experiencing some form of hair loss. Reasons vary. They include inherited female pattern baldness, stress reactions, medical conditions such as **Alopecia**—abnormal hair loss—traumatic burn injuries, and hair loss resulting from chemotherapy.

These women aren't just having an occasional bad-hair day. As their appearance changes, their self-confidence deteriorates. They're upset, anxious, frustrated, and discouraged. Their self-esteem is compromised and their sense of identity is sabotaged. Some become clinically depressed. Some actually stop going out of the house. On top of that, this generation of women was taught to care more than their predecessors about their appearance, partly due to the advancements experienced by women in today's society along with the importance put on image in today's world. The situation is compounded by an overall reluctance to address the subject. Because of these factors, there is now a serious need for expert advice and training on the subject.

Hair loss wasn't always at the forefront of my own life. After training in Europe, I became a high-profile salon stylist. I was on stage with Vidal Sassoon and Paul Mitchell. I styled the Saudi Arabian royal family, Vogue models, and the President of the United States. Then my nine-year-old niece learned that she had cancer. "Uncle Jeff," she said, "don't let me lose my hair." She was about to try out for gymnastics and I promised her she would be able to perform without having to worry about how she looked.

I had made wigs in Europe as part of my training, but the wig I needed to produce for my niece was not going to be a fashion wig—it needed to be designed for a child and it needed to stay on through anything. With the help of a manufacturer and various specialists, we were able to create the right wig for my niece, and she performed like a star. Seeing the joy on her face at her moment of accomplishment enlightened me in a completely new way, and I experienced an awakening of purpose, both in my career and in my life.

Six months later, I opened the doors of a cosmetic therapy center. On that day, my mother and my sister were diagnosed with cancer. In the ensuing months, I learned a great deal about the compassion that is needed to help someone who is dealing with a life-threatening disease as well as hair loss. In the coming years, I would learn even more from a multitude of clients.

Once the media caught onto what we were doing with our hair-loss treatments, everything exploded. I began hearing about children who needed wigs but couldn't afford them, so we set up a nonprofit organization, Wigs For Kids. Over the years, our organization has helped thousands. We've never turned away a child.

I have worked with thousands of female clients—including girls as young as five years old—on their hair thinning and hair loss concerns. I have been the "fly on the wall" of the metaphorical private locker room, where a woman's initial inquiries about her hair loss are at first tentatively whispered. Many women have told me that losing their hair was as traumatic as the loss of any other body part would be. I have seen time and time again how a woman's life is radically changed for the worse due to hair loss, and then I have seen it get dramatically better after a skillful hair restoration.

In a discussion with my colleague Dr. Matt Leavitt, the founder of Medical Hair Restoration and a leading expert in the industry, I asked what he thought the future held for our clients. I asked him this question because he is continually in the throes of research and education regarding hair restoration, with an emphasis on surgical, topical, and pharmaceutical solutions. He answered in a way that made me feel genuinely good about our work and mission at Beautiful Hair, where we focus on what we call a Total Approach to restoring a woman's hair. This approach is an integral part of this book.

"The future of hair restoration will involve a total approach, where patients have all treatment options," Dr. Leavitt said. "Now, if you walk into a surgical office, they will offer you surgery. Or if you walk into a salon, they will offer you styling and a few other options. But as we become educators, we will be able to offer clients all the options they need."

My wife, Zina, and I started the Jeffrey Paul Institute (the only independent, non-manufacturer, education and research firm to address hair loss) more than 20 years ago with a mission to restore beautiful hair using just this type of total approach. We conducted seminars geared toward educating people about hair loss issues and solutions. We established a mentoring program through which hair-care professionals could intern at the Institute and learn about hair loss as they worked. We conducted technical analyses and tested products in our laboratories, trained students and then retrained them as alumniae, and made a point of keeping graduates up to date with the latest developments in hair restoration through our newsletter and further training.

We created the Restoring Beautiful Hair Program specifically for men, women, and children who needed additional hair. Over the years, we have worked to help our clients regain self-confidence through the restoration of their hair, because we have always understood what they innately know—that their hair is a vital element of personal identity. We are simultaneously passionate and compassionate about the problem because that is what solving it requires. Our commitment to the problem of hair loss—especially among women—has provided us with years of professional expertise, which we want to share.

I have written another book for women experiencing hair loss that educates the consumer from a sensitive and informative level: *Beautiful Hair: Real Life Solutions To Women's Hair Thinning And Hair Loss*. It is my hope that educating women experiencing these problems and the professionals who treat them will result in a major step forward in our field. By being better informed, you will do better work and gain clients, and your clients will live better lives. Women dealing with hair thinning and loss need effective solutions, and they constitute an expanding market that salon professionals cannot afford to disregard. With their ranks growing by 10 percent a year, more women are looking for help every day, and more of them have the buying power to get it.

Unfortunately, too few hair care professionals have the knowledge and skills to help these women. Providers who have not been trained to identify and deal with women's hair loss cannot advise or assist their clients. They also cannot expect to retain their share of the market. Driven by need, their clients will seek satisfaction elsewhere and move on.

But there is no reason for you as a hair care professional to lose your share of this market—just as your clients do not need to continue to suffer. Solutions are available. Hair-replacement techniques designed to meet a variety of needs and budgets have reached a high level of refinement. What is needed are professionals trained in these techniques who can help women struggling with hair loss to find the solutions that meet their needs.

You can get the training to help these women and provide them with terrific solutions to restore their self-esteem while improving your business. I have written this book for you and your potential clients. It is a viable tool to get you started, help you build your hair restoration and replacement business, and establish another soothing place where women undermined by hair thinning and loss can turn.

In this book, I share much of my life's experience with you to help you reach women who are losing their hair. We begin with a definition of the qualities of healthy natural hair, proceed to the reasons for women's hair thinning and hair loss, and then take you step by step through several hair replacement options, from the initial assessment through the design process to the delivery of the final product. My hope is that with the detailed descriptions of every step of each hair restoration technique, you will be able to carry out the work of restoring beautiful hair, or train others so your business will grow.

Beauty is not only skin deep. If you are ready to take on this new endeavor, you will not only be turning toward booming business and restoring hair. You will also be helping women to look their best, reviving not only their appearances, but their spirits. I believe this is the key to real transformation.

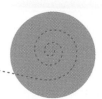

BEAUTIFUL HAIR:
What It Is, Where It Went, and How to Give It Back

Before you can begin to treat any problem, you must first understand what makes it a problem and how to provide the best possible resolution. In the case of hair thinning and hair loss, it is important to know what makes beautiful hair beautiful before attempting to restore that beauty to the person who is losing it or has lost it.

In this book, you will learn about the many factors that contribute to an individual client's idea of attractiveness. Then you will learn what makes hair thin and fall out, so that you have a complete understanding of what clients are facing during your work with them. Next you will examine everything you need to know about restoring hair and the components of restoring hair, so you have a foundation from which to work. Finally, I will walk you through each of 10 potential solutions to hair restoration and replacement, giving you the step-by-step instructions you will need to do everything from styling thin hair to applying extensions and providing laser treatment, and much more. All of this background information is presented to equip you with everything you need to know about restoring and replacing beautiful hair for those in need of your invaluable expertise.

Acknowledgments

Book Contributors

Dr. Larry L. Bosley
Bosley Medical Hair Restoration

Dr. Matt Leavitt
Founder of Medical Hair Restoration

Kevin Mancuso
Author of *The Mane Thing*

Dr. Susan Craig Scott
New York Dermatologist
Author of the *Hair Bible*

Dr. Pradi Mirmirani
The Hair Research Center
The University of California

Dr. Vera Price
The Hair Research Center
The University of California

Dr. Geoffrey Redmond
Director of Hormone Health Center
New York, NY

Chrissy Vitallo
Founder of Chrissy V Cold Bond
   System

Dr. Wilma Bergfeld
Former President of American Academy
   of Dermatology

Head of Dermatology Research
Cleveland Clinic Foundation

Okyo Sthair
New Concepts

Darla Smith
Vice President of Technical Services
   at International Hairgoods

Gary Ross
Contributor to *Healthy Hair Magazine*

Women's Institute of Fine and
   Thinning Hair
Rogaine for Women

Robin Knight
Extension Specialist

Salvatore Megna
Founder and President of Mega Hair

Isaac Bracha
Owner and President of Hair and
   Compound, Inc.

Isa Lefkowitz
President of Isa Designs

Robert Anzivino
President of Look of Love Company

Charlotte Jayne
Co-founder/Executive Vice President
 of Garland & Drake

Dr. Paul Riggs
Clinic Director
Coastal Medical Group

Dr. Dominic Brandy
The Medical Hair Institute

Dawn Harrison
President, Invisible Hairs

Andy Wright
On-Rite Company

Ovian Berg
Harmonix Corporation

Karen Hurguy
Graphic Artist

Joe Ferline
Photographer

Lou from Lusso Cosmetics
Photographer

ABOUT THE AUTHOR

JEFFREY PAUL began his career as a talented salon stylist, training at the Espam schools throughout Europe and serving as education director and international guest artist for Roffler Industries. During his years as a salon stylist, Jeffrey worked with Sassoon and Paul Mitchell, among others; his highly diverse clientele included the queen of Saudi Arabia, Vogue models, professional athletes and entertainers, and even a president of the United States. He founded Framesi U.S.A., the Data Design Academy, and the Hair Cutting Club. He has been a guest educator at all the major beauty shows in the United States and Europe and has coordinated fashion shows for Framesi and *Playboy* magazine.

Paul's attention was first focused on hair restoration and replacement when his young niece, a leukemia patient, lost her hair from chemotherapy and turned to him for help. When Paul could not find a child's hairpiece of acceptable quality, he decided to make one himself. In the process, he discovered his life's mission: to serve the physical and emotional needs of individuals who have been scarred by disease, injury, or trauma. Paul believes that when people feel good about how they look, they feel better about themselves, and that such a feeling is crucial to healing. His goal is to help each and every client regain their self-confidence.

In 1981 Paul and his wife, Zina, who is also a gifted hair designer, transformed their Rocky River, Ohio, salon and spa into a center for hair replacement and restoration. While their work with individual clients is closest to their hearts, they also conduct research; test products, materials, and methods; and design and create hair replacement systems and product lines. They have become known nationally and internationally as leaders in the field of hair restoration and replacement.

Paul serves as a consultant to a number of different industries. Major hairpiece manufacturers frequently call upon his expertise. He has advised hair replacement companies from Milan to Hollywood, developing educational programs and creating new materials and designs. He has served on the board of directors of the American Hair Loss Council. The Cleveland Clinic Foundation's prosthesis department called upon him to find a way to create a cosmetically acceptable appearance for patients needing prosthetic eyebrows, eyelashes, mustaches, and sideburns. The American Cancer Society and major medical centers throughout northeast Ohio refer their patients to him. Paul has been instrumental in setting up hair replacement and cosmetic reconstruction clinics in burn units of medical centers throughout the country. He regularly conducts seminars and workshops for salon and spa professionals in the United States and Canada, teaching the latest techniques for hair restoration and replacement.

Paul has been a frequent guest on radio and television news programs and talk shows, both local and nationwide. He has been the subject of countless newspaper and magazine articles.

He has served as editor of the National Hair Journal and has written articles for many trade publications in the hair care industry. He is a dynamic and popular public speaker and frequently lectures to both community and professional groups on the subject of hair restoration and replacement.

In 1983 Jeffrey and Zina Paul founded Wigs for Kids, a nonprofit organization that provides custom-made hair replacement systems at no cost to children who lose their hair for medical reasons. Over the years Wigs for Kids has provided thousands of children with hairpieces. No child has ever been turned away. (Further information on Wigs for Kids may be found at www.wigsforkids.org.)

About the Author

BEAUTIFUL HAIR—
What It Is

CHAPTER

1

INTRODUCTION

Before you can restore beautiful hair, you need to know what it is. For that, you need look no further than to a typical twelve-year-old girl. Her head of healthy, beautiful hair has five specific elements that combine to give it that unmistakable beauty:

- shine and condition
- shade and color
- texture and wave
- style and framing
- growth

These five components comprise the qualities necessary for beautiful hair. Duplicating or simulating them successfully is the goal of hair restoration.

THE CROWNING GLORY:
What Makes Hair Royally Beautiful

As you already are well aware from your work, hair serves a purpose beyond its strictly biological function of keeping us protected or warm. Hair is used to make a statement about our style, to attract people, to make good first impressions, to have fun, and to make us feel good about ourselves.

Women change their hair color, cosmetic texture, cut, and style in order to get an immediate boost in self-esteem. When the going gets tough, the tough change their hair. A woman on a bad-hair day doesn't feel like herself. A woman who needs to feel better about herself heads straight for the salon. Having beautiful hair means much more than simply looking good—it makes us feel great.

Madonna knows this. For years, her hair changes have mesmerized us. From long and loose to short and spiky, to bouncy blonde, to blunt, to genie-like, to dark and sleek, to comfortably casual, her hair has evolved along with her art to maintain our interest. Cher knows this, too. She goes from black to auburn, to fiery red, to platinum blonde, from natural to wig. She uses hair as an accessory and admits that it helps her show her fun side and feel her vitality. Jennifer Aniston also knows it. She hit a popular nerve with her first *Friends* 'do and varied it as it grew, but, along with her talents, her hairdo helped make and keep her a star.

Women around the world realize the effect of hair, proven by their frequent visits to salons and hair therapy spas for treatments that sometimes only they notice, but that make them feel like a million dollars. But hair is not just an accessory; it's a working tool for women. Starlets on the silver screen have tossed it in the direction of their romantic interests, grabbed it in horror, tousled it in confusion, chopped it in defiance, or kept it stylishly under wraps as they sped across America in a convertible to escape the men who traumatized them.

No other accessory has proven that it can say so much. Our hair has to look good in order for us to feel good and so

Potential Clients Answer the Question: What Makes Hair Beautiful to You?

Beautiful hair to me is lustrous, and full of shine. The grass is always greener on the other side, so straight-haired people want curly hair and vice versa. But if hair looks clearly natural and has a certain body to it, and it frames and flatters the face, that's admirable. Hair should complement the face and enhance the person's image. It shouldn't stand out or be ostentatious. I think there is beauty in both straight and curly hair, and you should just work with what God gave you.

—Ida, experiencing age- and stress-related hair loss, 80 years old, New York

that we can make the most of it, whatever situation arises. We need to know we have that tool to help us be our best in every circumstance.

But it can't be hair that just sits there. What makes hair come alive? What is it about beautiful hair that makes us so happy when we have it? We've all seen it: lustrous, silky sleek or animatedly curly, color-rich manes on models gracing the covers of magazines or flitting flirtingly across our television screens.

What is the promise of beautiful hair that drives women into our salons? What are those elements of beauty that are coveted, even by those who have all of their

Beautiful Hair—What It Is

> ## Potential Clients Answer the Question: What Makes Hair Beautiful To You?
>
> Hair that is long and curly is sexy. It looks like time was spent on it to make it look good. If it's clean and bouncy it looks complex and exciting. Gray hair is not beautiful—hair with strong color, whether blonde, dark brown or black, is particularly attractive. Yes, I may understand what it's like to lose my hair, but that doesn't make me appreciate beautiful hair any less.
>
> —*Scott, experiencing hereditary male pattern receding,*
> *34 years old, Oklahoma*

hair? We need to understand this fully and remember it if we are to be successful in providing service to our clients at all times.

When we are drawn to how terrific hair looks, it's for five very specific reasons.

First, we notice the hair's *shine*. Healthy hair has many facets and—just like a prism—it gleams when light catches it. When you see those glimmering glints dancing through hair, you know immediately that it is in extremely good condition. It may remind you of conditioner commercials that show shiny hair spreading out in slow motion across a shoulder.

Second, we see *color*, not just one color, but a half-dozen or more that are naturally blended together to create a beautiful head of hair. This individualized blend of color—light and dark, bright and dull, subdued and rich—helps create a sense of density and over-all texture. Think Russo red and Monroe blonde.

Third, our eyes register the **texture**. Texture encompasses the wave, movement, body, and density of hair. Texture is determined, more or less, by the amount and type of hair a person has. Celebrities often induce the texture of their hair through styling to emulate other textures.

There are four overall texture categories. Straight hair hugs the scalp as it emerges from the hair follicle, and usually has an outer cuticle that lies snugly against the hair shaft. It's exactly what its description says it is—hair with no curl or wave. However, its very nature gives it its stunning appearance. Because the cuticle is flat on the hair shaft, straight hair usually has lots of natural shine and body.

Wavy hair, like straight hair, hugs the scalp as it grows out. Its long S-shaped curl gives it exceptional manageability and volume, which makes it the easiest of all hair types to style, according to Kevin Mancuso, New York-based hair stylist and author of *The Mane Thing*. Yet, the majority of people do not have hair that falls into this category.

Beautiful Hair—What It Is

Potential Clients Answer the Question: What Makes Hair Beautiful To You?

If a woman has long hair past her shoulders, with lots of body so you can run your fingers through it, that's beautiful. It's not beautiful if it's thin and stringy.

—*Adam, experiencing early stages of male pattern loss,*
22 years old, Illinois

If hair looks healthy—thick, shiny, and well groomed—that's beautiful hair I would do anything for.

—*Emma, experiencing hair thinning from stress,*
60 years old, Florida

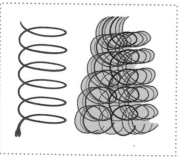

Curly hair grows out and away from the scalp and has a tighter S-shaped curl that creates lots of volume, which makes it high-maintenance hair, says Mancuso. There is an upside to all that volume, however. It's called versatility. "Where straight hair might need product texturizing to give it volume and pliability, curly hair has those attributes naturally," he says. That means it's very easy to style.

Kinky hair runs the gamut—from very fine to very course individual hairs. It usually has "fantastic sheen" says Mancuso, and offers a lot of styling options. The downside of kinky hair? "It is usually very dense," says Mancuso, "and can trap oil and dead skin against the scalp." That is why it is important to wash it on a regular basis.

The fourth quality we notice in beautiful hair has to do with its *framing*, or its effect on your face. From the shortest crop to the longest pageboy, hair that is properly cut and styled to complement bone structure, features, and coloring can transform appearance. While the cut and shape of the hair may be striking, the style will be most effective when it does not overshadow the beauty it surrounds—your face.

Finally, when we see a head of beautiful hair, we are seeing something so basic we probably don't even think about it. We are noticing healthy *growth*—in other words, the hair's history. Healthy growth is due to many things: good genes; good circulation that brings nutrient-rich blood to the scalp; a healthy diet (with or without nutritional supplements) that provides the building blocks—vitamins, minerals, amino acids—for healthy hair; and a hair-care regimen that incorporates products, tools, and techniques that are good for hair, such as conditioners, natural bristle brushes, and scalp massage, rather than those that are not, such as bleaches, curling irons, and ratting or back-combing.

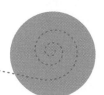

WHEN THE FIVE ELEMENTS FALTER

What's Possible?

But what if hair won't grow or grows only to a certain point and then breaks off? Without growth there is no shine, the color is dull, the hair is lifeless, and it neither frames nor flatters the face. Or what if hair sheds so that the scalp shows through? What if hair has been lost due to head trauma, stress-related **Alopecia Areata**—the sudden falling out of hair in round patches

8

Potential Clients Answer the Question: What Makes Hair Beautiful To You?

I like Britney Spears' hair. It's long and shiny, and she can wear it curly or straight. I wish my hair was like that.

—Jesse, thin hair, 11 years old, Florida

Long and shiny, well groomed, neat, flowing hair is beautiful, attractive hair. Like my wife's hair when I first met her.

—Rob, experiencing male pattern hair loss, 63 years old, New York

or baldness in spots—female pattern baldness, or chemotherapy treatments for cancer?

Is achieving the look and feel of beautiful hair an impossible dream? In the past, it was. But today, because of the technology, expertise, and materials that are available, hair restoration professionals are making the dream a reality on a routine basis. These professionals, whom I prefer to call cosmetic therapists, offer products and treatments that can help improve the look, quality, and performance of damaged hair and hair that refuses to grow. They offer help in choosing, fitting, and styling hair additions to replace hair that has been lost. The right professionals can form a dynamic and experienced cosmetic therapy team to help clients overcome their hair loss concerns. This book will help you become a cosmetic therapist, and will help you understand all you need to know to restore your clients' beautiful hair.

Going Outside of Nature to
Regain or Obtain Beautiful Hair

There are a lot of different ways you can treat hair loss. I will touch on them briefly here and describe them in detail later in this book. You can treat the scalp or teach your clients to treat their scalps with products designed to help stimulate growth and promote the health of the scalp. You can style existing hair differently to cover loss in a way that makes the client feel more comfortable. You can camouflage areas of the scalp that have begun to show through where hair has been lost. You can duplicate the beautiful natural look—the shine, color, texture, frame, and growth—of lost hair with a substitute: replacement hair.

A world of options awaits. It may seem like a fairy tale to your clients when you help them discover the best answer to their hair concerns, because the results can indeed be magical.

Potential Clients Answer the Question:
What Makes Hair Beautiful To You?

I always notice hair that is shiny, that has fullness and an apparent ease of style. It's hair that can't help but look like it's in great shape, like Liv Tyler's or Jennifer Aniston's.

—*Cynthia, experiencing medically related hair loss, 35 years old, California*

Others on Your Side

In the companion book, geared toward client education on restoring their hair and/or choosing replacement options, I list types of experts clients may turn to for guidance in dealing with their concerns. The list will help clients form a small team of professionals to address those concerns. It will be clear to the client reading the book that you—the cosmetic therapist or hair restoration and replacement professional—are the nucleus of that team. The book also indicates that the client is the team leader, accepting guidance, but using personal powers of discernment to come to the right solution. Nevertheless, your particular guidance here will be crucial. (I recommend that you read the companion book to familiarize yourself with information your clients are reading.)

There are other professionals whose advice may come into play, and you should be prepared to hear about them and respect their expertise in dealing with your clients. This is important in reaching well-rounded conclusions about which solutions may be best for your clients, and in establishing your clients' trust of your ability to carefully evaluate their needs and desires.

Potential Clients Answer the Question: What Makes Hair Beautiful To You?

If a woman has long, silky, well-conditioned, clean, non-greasy hair, it's the most beautiful hair there is.

—Neal, experiencing early stages of male pattern baldness, 41 years old, New York

Potential Clients Answer the Question: What Makes Hair Beautiful To You?

I envy any woman who is lucky enough to have a full head of hair. For me, that's all the beauty I would ask for.

—Sara, experiencing acute female pattern baldness, 26 years old, New York

These professionals may be doctors, therapists, nutritionists, or others. Use your judgment, but note that your clients may have great respect for the advice they received from others, and you should factor in that advice for their comfort where appropriate. Finally, as you do with your styling services, remember that once your clients have heard your input and understood the options, the ultimate decision is still theirs.

It will be helpful to you to understand what causes hair loss and to learn the basics of the problem before you assess your clients. Let's take a look at those details, and then we'll move on to the evaluation process and the life-altering solutions.

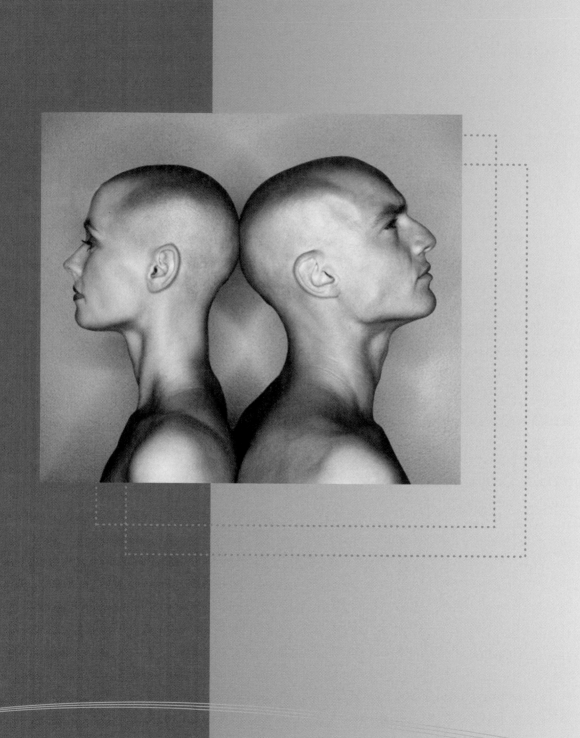

BEAUTIFUL HAIR—
Where It Went

CHAPTER
2

DIS-TRESS: Causes of Women's Hair Thinning and Loss

By taking the time to understand the causes of the problem, we can begin to consider the solutions for relieving a client's distress. Hair thinning and loss can be attributed to many factors, and often combinations of those factors. Generally speaking, they may include:

- genetic predisposition (a family history of hair loss)
- stress and trauma (constriction of blood supply; poor vitamin assimilation)
- nutrition and diet (high consumption of animal fats)
- health issues (thyroid imbalance)
- medications (chemotherapy)
- environment (pseudo-estrogens and pseudo-androgens)
- chemical damage (incorrect chemical processes applied to hair)

Most of these factors lead to a miniaturization of hair, when hair follicle deterioration caused by pollutants or toxins causes individual hairs to become smaller and finer, until the follicle remains in the telogen (resting) phase and is totally dormant. This means that the hair follicle begins to shrink, and the life expectancy of hair diminishes. When hair does grow, it grows over a shorter period of time, becomes finer and less pigmented, and finally stops growing. Eventually the hair follicle atrophies and growth stops completely. An exception to this is in the case of **Alopecia Areata**, in which the condition of the scalp—rather than the condition of the hair follicles themselves—leads to the loss of hair.

Dr. Matt Leavitt, founder of Medical Hair Restoration and former vice president of the American Board of Hair Restoration Surgery, calls the hair experiencing miniaturization "wimpy hair" that people automatically assume is thinning and falling out. In reality, he says, the hair is narrowing. Miniaturized hairs are fragile, susceptible to any sort of trauma, and susceptible to falling out even if someone has a bad flu. Further loss of miniaturized hair can be triggered by environmental factors and surgery. Women, more than men, experience easy loss of miniaturized hair—what is called "shock loss"—around areas of their head during surgical treatment, according to Leavitt, who specializes in surgical solutions to hair loss. Their hair thins, and when it thins enough, it becomes vulnerable to being lost.

Usually, when women begin to lose their hair or notice a difference in the thickness and strength of their hair, they decide it must have to do with either aging or some external factor like stress or oncoming illness. Sometimes these are the causes, but there are many possibilities. Read the following descriptions of causes of hair thinning and loss carefully to begin to identify, with your clients, the potential causes of their loss of hair. Once you have identified the probable causes of the hair loss (usually there is more than one) and the degree to which the loss has progressed, you can look at the solutions in this book and decide which one or which combination is best or where to direct a client for additional services.

The following are direct causes of hair loss:

Androgenetic Alopecia: This is hereditary hair thinning, which expresses itself in a different pattern for women than it does for men. An estimated 30 million women have this problem. Generally they experience a gradual, diffused thinning over the top of their heads or the crowns of their heads while often keeping their frontal hairline. The Women's Institute for Fine and Thinning Hair states that more than 70% of women experiencing hair loss and thinning may attribute it to **Androgenetic Alopecia**. An estimated 50 million men have this problem. They experience "male pattern baldness," which takes the form of receding hairlines and balding across the top of the head, pushing backward over the scalp.

Alopecia Areata: This is brought on by an immune system disorder in which hair follicles abruptly stop growing hair, resulting in patches of baldness or thinning. What is actually happening is that when the hair grows, it appears white in the center and regains color as it gets longer. One of the most common forms is complete loss of hair on the head in a circular patch about 1–10 centimeters in diameter. In **Alopecia Areata,** hair loss that is triggered by stress will sometimes grow back after the stress is cured. In other cases, treatment is necessary. Complete baldness is rare. The psychological damage associated with **Alopecia Areata** is the most damaging aspect of the condition since it is sudden and unexpected. **Alopecia Areata** tends to be apparent in families with a history of asthma, eczema, or autoimmune disorders such as rheumatoid arthritis or lupus erythematosus.

Anagen Effluvium: Effluvium is a medical term meaning hair loss. In this case, hair is lost due to internally administered medications, like chemotherapy agents that poison the hair follicle.

Involutional Alopecia: In this case, your hair follicles become dormant, and the hairs that are left become shorter and sparser due to the natural aging process.

Telogen Effluvium: This is similar to **Androgenetic Alopecia** with more generalized thinning, but it begins more quickly and is only a temporary condition since its cause is usually a sudden stress or illness that shocks the system and makes hair fall out for a time. This shedding can be triggered by a variety of emotional or physical stresses, including mental illness, rapid weight change, poor diet, surgery, anemia, death of a loved one, thyroid abnormalities, excessive amounts of vitamin A or blood pressure medicine, and hormonal changes due to pregnancy, birth control, or menopause.

Traumatic Alopecia: The classic example of what overuse of damaging styling products and reshapers (like hot combs and relaxing agents) can do to hair growth, it is widely experienced by African-American women and women who use extensions and braiding techniques repeatedly over a long time period. There are specific categories of this, including **Traction Alopecia,** which results from tight rollers and braiding and looks like serious thinning over the ears and at an increasingly receding hairline; **Chemical Alopecia,** which results from commercial relaxers and shows itself in scalp scarring combined with a hereditary loss pattern; and **Follicular Degeneration Syndrome,** which results from the continual use of pomades with hot irons and combs and looks distinctly like a symmetrical scarring beginning at the crown of the head and progressing evenly.

Friction Alopecia: This is hair breakage and hair that is pulled from the follicles due to consistent friction from tight hats and wigs.

Cheerleading Propecia: Conveniently dubbed, this type of loss is a warning to all girls that high school is truly over. Persistent ponytail wearers, especially those who wear them tightly and with bands that pull individual hairs, may have conditioned their scalps for trouble. Over time, those tight tails will translate into breakage and lost hair near the hairline and over the ears. This begins to look like slight to sharp dips at the outer edges of the upper hairline and fuzzy, flyaway tufts of hair that appear over ears when your hair is tied back.

Many factors bring about these kinds of hair conditions, most of which are described above. Others include hormonal shifts due to the outset of a chronic disease, constriction of blood supply, poor vitamin assimilation, use of medications, heredity, traditional or fashionable hair styling methods, damage from incorrect chemical processing, anesthesia, environmental influences, and a host of endocrine and metabolic changes.

Experts have their own opinions of which factors are most prevalent based on their experiences with female clients dealing with hair loss. According to Dr. Susan Craig Scott, a New York based dermatologist who is a former board member on the American Hair Loss Council and author of *The Hair Bible*, the most common cause of hair loss is genetic predisposition. But, she says, hair loss specialists are taking diet and nutrition (or

Crash Dieters and Anemics

Dr. Robert M. Bernstein, director of the New Hair Institute in New York City and in Fort Lee, New Jersey, cites crash diets and anemia as two potential underlying factors on a long list of those that may contribute to hair loss and that should be ruled out by medical evaluation before embarking on finding the right solution. Limiting nutrients by crash dieting or dieting too severely can rob hair follicles of what they need to survive. If your clients are experiencing thinning or loss and have been crash dieting, advise them to change to a nutritionally sound program as quickly as possible and to follow up with a nutritionist or doctor. If they have shared that they are anemic, advise them to get enough iron, which has a strong impact on hair's good health. They should certainly see their doctor or nutritionist for the recommended dosage of iron for their circumstances.

lack of certain nutrients) more seriously than they have in the past, particularly because of the current interest in consuming very little fat in our diets. "We need to make sure that a good portion of our daily diet is fat—about 20 percent of our caloric intake," Scott says. "A diet way too low in fat can result in thinning and loss." A diet too high in fat may also contribute to hair loss.

According to Dr. Matt Leavitt, hair is produced by a follicle under the scalp, and as we get older the follicle ages too. The living, but aging, follicle then causes thinner hair. Dr. Leavitt says that oral contraceptives and medication can cause hair loss, but noticing the effects of taking, changing, or stopping medication can take more than a year, so a correlation between hair loss and thinning and the medicine may be difficult to find.

"Patients say, 'It can't be the medication, because I've been taking it for a while and nothing's happened to my hair in all that time,' but they don't get the connection because of the time span between when they start on the drug and when they notice their hair loss," says Dr. Leavitt.

Dr. Paradi Mirmirani of the Hair Research Center at the University of California, San Francisco, and Dr. Vera Price have worked with African-American female clients, many of whom have experienced hair loss patterns caused by heredity and longtime styling methods. Dr. Price has identified causes of hair loss among African-American clients in three categories:

1. hereditary thinning, which usually takes the form of an exaggerated reshaping of the frontal hairline as well as diffuse thinning atop the scalp

2. traction alopecia (as described above), in which front and side hair is lost because of hair being pulled backward in tight braids, weaves, cornrows, and extensions for many years

3. the inability of hair to grow long caused by breakage. Over many years of using various products, hair often approaches the point where it can no longer take the pressure it could earlier in life.

African-American women make up the great majority of wig buyers and extension wearers, and have for many years. Information presented to this group at an early age might lessen the amount of pull and frequency of heat styling that contributes to hair loss and, thus, promote a lifetime of healthy hair care practice.

Menopause and Estrogen

Dr. Geoffrey Redmond, an endocrinologist specializing in female hormonal problems and Director of the Hormone Help Center in New York, is one of the few experts to have addressed menopause as a cause of hair loss. Dr. Redmond claims that one of the most stressful side effects of menopause is **Alopecia,** since menopause is a time in a woman's life marked by decreased estrogen levels.

"Estrogen helps hair," says Dr. Redmond. "It does this by lengthening the hair cycle so that each hair stays on the head longer—resulting in thicker hair." Dr. Redmond says that estrogen-deficiency **Alopecia** generally starts near the onset of menopause and, because estrogen levels start to fall before a woman's menstrual cycle actually halts, this form of Alopecia may, for some women, be the first sign of approaching menopause.

"I show my patients their magnified hair, under a microscope, in the hope that it will leave the lasting impression with them that they need to consider how to prevent further damage by changing their hair care habits and educating others around them to do the same whenever possible," says Dr. Mirmirani. Drs. Mirmirani and Price also work closely with many HIV-positive clients who experience hair thinning due to the progression and stages of their disease.

Hair Life Cycle

Now that we have discussed the different types of hair loss and the causes that trigger them, let's take a look at how hair grows normally so that we can understand non-growth more comprehensively.

Hair is dynamic. The part of the hair shaft that you can actually see is the dead part. It's the "end" product of a growth process that is going on beneath the surface, under the skin of the scalp. But the part of the hair shaft you don't see is alive and kicking, responding to the forces within our bodies, the environment outside our bodies, and a host of other things.

I like to use trees as examples of how alive hair is. A tree trunk has three main layers. The densest part of the trunk is the pith, or heartwood. Sapwood is the next layer, which keeps the

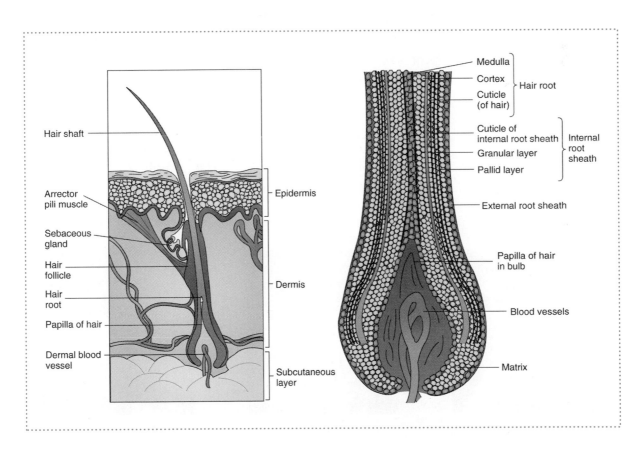

Beautiful Hair—Where It Went

tree supplied with nutrients and supports its upward growth, and the bark is the outer layer, which acts as a protective barrier.

Hair has three major layers, too. There's the medulla, which is the innermost lifeline that feeds the hair; the cortex, which gives the hair shaft its width and color; and the cuticle, which, like bark, acts as the outer protective barrier. All grow out of a hair follicle that nourishes the hair shaft, but thrives beneath the scalp's skin.

Trees have hard-working roots that do two things. They anchor the tree into the earth, and they reach out into the surrounding soil and absorb the water and nutrients that the tree needs in order to grow.

Hairs have hard-working papillae. They help anchor the hair shaft firmly into the head and furnish nourishment to the hair shaft through the tiny blood vessels and capillaries that are loosely connected to it.

Tree bark is rough and scaly—suitable for its important job of acting as the armor that protects the softer, inner wood of the tree. Hair shaft cuticle is rough also, and opens outward in scales comprised of up to 97 percent protein matter—similarly suitable for its job of acting as the armor that protects the cortex and medulla of the hair shaft.

 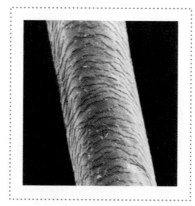 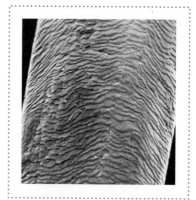

Finally, trees need to be pruned and trimmed to keep them looking their best. So does hair. I tell my clients who visit my hair restoration center, and attendees of the conferences, workshops, and symposiums where I teach, and readers of the publications for which I write, that hair is not dead. It is constantly growing, reacting to the environment, and changing on us. Since we don't know of anything dead that does all that, we should consider hair to be full of life.

Blondes have, on average, about 140,000 scalp hairs; brunettes have about 105,000; and redheads have about 90,000. Some people are born with finely textured hair, which, at a mere 50 microns in diameter (about one-fourth of the size of the period at the end of this sentence), tends to be fairly fragile. Others are born with coarse hair, which at 100-plus microns in diameter can take its fair share of abuse.

Some people are born with curly hair, some with straight hair. The amount of curl in hair is the result of the shape of the hair shaft as it emerges from the hair follicle. Curly hair comes out fairly flat. Wavy hair comes out oval-shaped. Straight hair comes out practically round. It's this initial emergence shape that dictates how the hairs will fall and integrate with one another to create overall texture.

No matter the number of hairs on the head or the hair's texture, healthy, normal hair has a regular grow-shed cycle of about 80 to 100 hairs a day. So a certain amount of "fall out" is a natural occurrence.

When everything is going as it should, there are three stages of the grow-shed cycle. The first is the **anagen stage,** which lasts from two to six years. During this stage, hair is firmly seated in the hair follicle, getting plenty of nourishment, and growing one-fourth to one-half inch a month. This happens with more frequency in our youth, and lessens as we age.

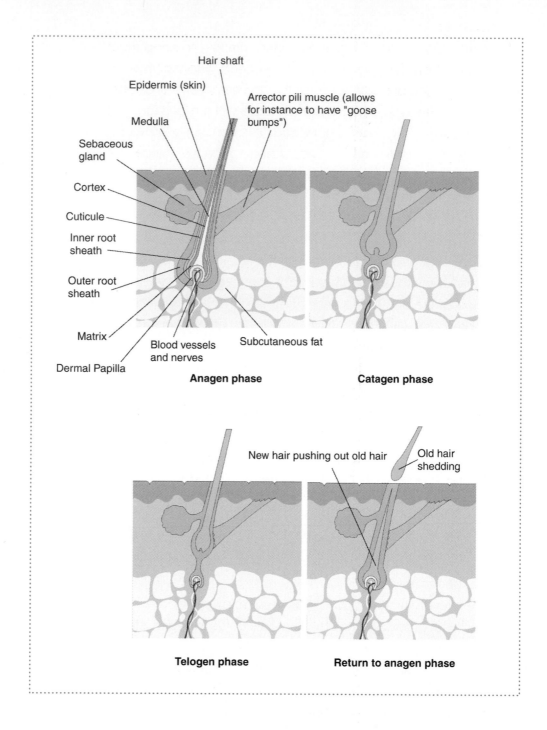

Hair shaft

Epidermis (skin)

Medulla

Arrector pili muscle (allows for instance to have "goose bumps")

Sebaceous gland

Cortex

Cuticule

Inner root sheath

Outer root sheath

Matrix

Blood vessels and nerves

Subcutaneous fat

Dermal Papilla

Anagen phase

Catagen phase

New hair pushing out old hair

Old hair shedding

Telogen phase

Return to anagen phase

"More than 85 percent of scalp hair is in this phase at any time," says dermatologist Dr. Wilma Bergfeld, former president of the American Academy of Dermatology and head of dermatology research at the Cleveland Clinic in Cleveland, Ohio. So, most hair is constantly in the process of feeding and growing.

The second is the **catagen stage,** which lasts from three to six weeks. During this stage, the hair root begins to separate from the hair shaft and nourishment falls off dramatically. As the hair shaft works its way out of the follicle, it is readying itself for shedding.

The third is the **telogen stage,** which lasts from three to five months. During this stage, nourishment for the "old" hair shaft has ceased, the hair follicle has gone into a resting stage, and hair falls—or is brushed or combed or washed—out. After a brief rest, the follicle re-enters the anagen stage, and the cycle begins again.

Normal shedding (as in **Telogen Effluvium,** described above) usually stops at some point, but not all shedding is normal, according to Dr. Bergfeld. There are many "triggers" that can lead to quickly increased shedding and partial or total hair loss (many of which we describe above). And according to Dr. Bergfeld, someone losing more than 100 hairs a day may have a hair loss condition.

No Need to Be a Math Whiz

Don't split hairs over the counting thing. "If [one is] observing more hairs in the shower drain, on clothes, or on bed pillows," explains Dr. Bergfeld, "then [they] may have a hair loss problem." The only sure way to know is to get a medical diagnosis

Myths About Hair and Hair Loss

"The notion that hair loss is caused by a single gene is an old wives' tale."

—Dr. Angela M. Christiano, Assistant Professor of Dermatology at Columbia University in New York, and lead researcher of a recent study that brought about the discovery of the human gene associated with hair loss, which is called Hairless.

Ironically, it's the silence on this subject that has brought forth so much speculative chatter about what makes hair "tick." The result? Myths that are believed without further question. Here is the truth to help dispel the myths:

- Dandruff does not cause hair loss.

- Oily hair (**seborrhea**) does not cause hair loss.

- Baseball caps, and hats in general, do not cause hair loss, but tight ones may lead to **Friction Alopecia**.

- Warm shower water does not cause hair loss—but hot water is not optimal.

- Cutting hair does not necessarily make it grow.

- Shaving one's head does not necessarily mean hair will then grow back curly.

- Hair thinning does not come from the mother's side of the family. Scientific research shows that it can come from either side. The best barometer is your immediate family. If members are losing their hair, you may also be at risk.

- Men are not the only ones who suffer from hereditary hair loss. Women do too. The difference is in patterns, with men losing and thinning in more concentrated areas, and women losing and thinning all over their heads.

- Women not only lose hair after pregnancy or during and after menopause.

- Women can begin to lose hair in their twenties.

- Stress won't make hair permanently fall out. It may fall out during stressful times in life, but when the stress dissipates, hair should grow back. It might cause hormonal shifts that would more likely be a direct effect of loss, though.

- If someone is losing some hair, it does not mean she is experiencing heredi-tary hair loss. Over 100 hairs can fall out daily during hair's natural "resting" (non-growing) phase. It's when hair is not in the resting phase and the hair does not return that a person may have a problem.

- If hair sticks around until the age of 40, it does not mean that it will stay forever. There is no cut-off date for potential loss of hair. It depends a lot on the genes.

- Hair loss treatments do not specifically cause sexual dysfunction.

- If people stop using certain hair loss treatments, their hair will not fall out even more than before. However, the process the treatment was beginning to keep at bay will reoccur. So they should continue to use the product as directed.

- Hair loss treatments can work if people use them correctly.

- Frequent shampooing will not make hair fall out. In fact, shampooing removes residues so that hair looks fuller (when dry, of course).

- Chemicals may weaken hair and cause hair to break, even close to the scalp. But that loss is temporary, unless—in rare cases—the follicle has been damaged by chemical treatment.

from a physician who specializes in hair loss, usually a dermatologist. Dr. Bergfeld claims the goal of a medical diagnosis is to correlate the amount of hair lost over time with the factors that are triggering the loss. With that understanding, an appropriate solution can be found.

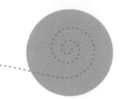

ASSESSING LEVELS OF LOSS: Identifying Diffusion Grade and Pattern Stage

The first step in hair restoration is to determine the area and degree of hair loss. Women's hair thinning and hair loss are classified into two categories: Diffusion and Pattern. Diffusion indicates the percentage of thinning or loss in the pattern area. Pattern represents the extent of the area of diminished hair on the head. The stages of FPB, or Female Pattern Baldness (a hereditary condition), are determined by how much of the head is affected by the area of hair loss.

Assigning values to Diffusion and Pattern measurements, called Diffusion Grades and Pattern Stages, is the first step to assessing levels of hair loss or thinning. You can then use these

Female Pattern Stages

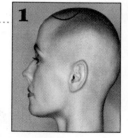 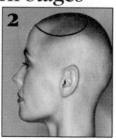 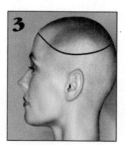 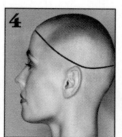 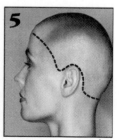

values to determine optimal solutions for your clients' concerns. To determine the Pattern Stage, look closely at your client's head to see which of the following five stages best describes the area of thinning or loss. While hair is wet, part hair from the top of the ear to the center of the top of the head (across). Look at how far the thinning comes down from the top of the part. You can use the following diagram to see how your client measures up.

Here are the Pattern Stages you can choose from as you determine your client's stage; this label will be useful while considering potential solutions later in this book:

Stage 1: Hair is thinning or gone close to the top and center of your client's head and forward, close to the hairline.

Stage 2: Hair loss or thinning extends almost to the back of the top part of your client's head and further sideways in a manner that would line up with the outer edges of their eyebrows if you drew a line from those edges up onto the scalp.

Stage 3: Hair thinning or loss extends to the back of the crown and sideways and down to an inch or two above your client's ear tops.

Stage 4: The affected area stretches from the back of the skull before it caves in to drop down to the nape of your client's neck and extends sideways and down to the tops of the ears.

Stage 5: All-over hair loss or thinning from the hairline to the nape of the neck, and surrounding the ear area completely.

Now take a close look at the Pattern Area, and see if you can tell which Grade of Diffusion best describes the extent of

Diffusion Evaluation

Top

Crown

Side

Grading Scale

Grade I	10% - 20%
Grade II	30% - 50%
Grade III	60% - 80%
Grade IV	90% - 100%

your client's thinning or loss. Again, while hair is still wet, take a good look at your client's scalp after you do the following: part hair down the middle from the front at the hairline all the way to the nape of the neck. Look at the hair closest to the nape of the neck (assuming this is close to normal growth levels) and estimate how much less, as a percentage, is at the top of your client's head in comparison with that hair.

Grade I—10–20 percent loss

Grade II—30–50 percent loss

Grade III—60–80 percent loss

Grade IV—90–100 percent loss

Different solutions described in this book will be more conducive to certain Diffusion Grades and Pattern Stages, and combinations thereof.

Give your client a Diffusion Grade:

_____.

Give your client a Pattern Stage:

_____.

These two values are the first to consider in evaluating the degree of hair thinning or loss and assessing the most appropriate solutions for your clients' hair restoration or replacement. But there are other indicators that will help as well, and we will examine them in our next chapter.

BEAUTIFUL HAIR—
Knowing the Woman Who Seeks It

The Consultation—The Personal Profile and Evaluation

CHAPTER 3

INTRODUCTION

At the core of the work of hair restoration is the personal profile, a methodical history and record of the client's background, hair type, face shape, skin tone, level of activity, preferences, and health treatment status. Through use of this inventory, you can determine the solution, or solutions, most appropriate for your clients. Learning to accurately assess and understand a client's situation is the key to finding a successful solution. The Personal Profile form presented in this book is designed to elicit maximum relevant information in the most concise fashion. It is important to familiarize yourself with the questions you will be asking your clients and to understand how their answers will help you deal with their hair loss issues.

You will also use a Consultation Profile to assess the condition of your client's hair and scalp, her baldness pattern stage, and her hair type. As the consultation continues, you and your client will determine what type of hair restoration will best suit her circumstances, way of life, and budget. You should also

B ｜ BEAUTIFUL HAIR™
Personal Profile

place photo here

Face Shapes

Consultant _____ Client Type _____ Date _____ Customer # _____

1. *Tell Us About Yourself*

Name _____ Date of Birth _____

Address _____ City _____ State _____ Zip _____

Home Phone _____ Work Phone _____ E-mail _____ Occupation _____

How were you referred to us? ☐ Medical Professional/Hospital ☐ Patient/Friend ☐ Salon ☐ Yellow Pages ☐ Web Page ☐ Media

Have you consulted with other professionals about hair replacement, restorations, or additions? ☐ Yes ☐ No

If yes, please give details

What is the main reason that brings you to our center? ☐ Fine or Thinning Hair (refer to Section 2) ☐ Camouflage ☐ Hair Extensions (refer to Section 2) ☐ Medical-related (refer to Section 3) ☐ Preventive Treatments ☐ Surgery

What is your lifestyle? ☐ Non-active ☐ Semi-active ☐ Active ☐ Athletic

Do you chemically process your hair? ☐ Professionally ☐ At home Explain Process: _____

Which of the following areas would you like to enhance? ☐ Volume/Fullness ☐ Texture/Wave ☐ Length ☐ Color

2. *Fine or Thinning Hair*

Women experience hereditary hair thinning at different stages. Some catch it early. Others go years before discovering their hair is thinning. Please take a moment to complete this survey and determine whether your hair is thinning.

Do you describe your hair as fine or thinning? ☐ Yes ☐ No If yes, how long have you been experiencing this? _____

Do you find that most styling products weigh your hair down? ☐ Yes ☐ No

Are you noticing more hair than usual in the shower drain, on your pillow, or in your hairbrush? ☐ Yes ☐ No

Have your family members experienced hair thinning or hair loss? ☐ Yes ☐ No Who: _____

Have you found that hair on top of your head grows in shorter than the rest of your hair? ☐ Yes ☐ No

Have you experienced irritation of the scalp? ☐ Yes ☐ No If yes, please explain. _____

3. *Medical-related Hair Loss*

Are you undergoing medical treatment? ☐ Yes ☐ No If yes, what type of treatment? _____

Have you already experienced hair loss? ☐ Yes ☐ No If yes, how long? _____

Doctor's Name _____

Hospital/Office Location _____

Have you had any allergic reactions? ☐ Yes ☐ No If yes, please indicate _____

Skin Matters

Learn how your hair color can work to brighten, complement, or correct your skin color. Skin tones fall into two families, warm and cool.

Warm Skin Tones: Brighten skin undertones by selecting hair colors with shades of red, gold, and true brown. Avoid shades of pale blonde or ash.

Cool Skin Tones: Warm and soften skin undertones with natural hair shades of ash, honey, and chestnut. Avoid strong reddish shades.

Oval

Square

Triangle

Round

Heart

Oblong

BEAUTIFUL **H**AIR™

— *Consultation Profile* —

History _____
_____
_____
_____

Assessment Analysis

Condition of growing hair & scalp _____
_____

Diffusion Grade _____ Pattern Stage _____

Face Shape _____ Color Tone _____

Recommended Solutions _____

Design Selection _____ *Design Size* _____

Hair Selection

Type _____ Texture _____

Attachment Selection _____
_____

Additional Solutions _____
_____

be informed about surgical hair restoration procedures and related considerations, even though you are not offering those services, so you will be able to recommend a qualified provider to a client.

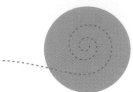

BEGINNING THE ASSESSMENT

Face Shape

Take a Polaroid head-and-shoulder shot of your client while her hair is pulled away from her face and hairline. Make sure the photo shows the full width of her shoulder span to put her face shape and position into perspective. Then take a black permanent marker and draw neatly and directly along the outline of her face in the photo. Hold it next to the diagram of face shape samples to determine which face shape she has. Most of us are combinations, but this will serve as a general guide.

Then look at this chapter's descriptions of styles to determine which is most flattering to your client's face shape and shoulder width, and which is most conducive to her lifestyle; decide which colors might be most complementary to her skin tone. Use this as a basis to explore further styling options.

WHEN HER FACE IS OVAL

Characteristics: Perfectly symmetrical.
The Goal: Don't worry, be happy!

Lucky girl. The oval face is the perfect face shape and its owner can wear almost any hairstyle. For long styles, a classic look is a center or side part with hair touching the shoulders. A short, layered look with curls and a close extended nape would work nicely too. Long, short, up, or in toward her face—they all look just right with her symmetrical face shape.

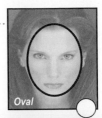

Oval

WHEN HER FACE IS SQUARE

Characteristics: Angular jaw, square brow, both nearly the same width
The Goal: Soften the sharp jaw angle and minimize her squared brow line

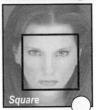

Square

Her style should lift off her forehead. If you brush it forward at the temples and jaw line, it will lend her face shape some necessary narrowness and softness. She can wear wispy bangs. Her face goes perfectly with asymmetrical styles, so she would have done well in the 1980s under new wave styles, some of which are back in vogue with a softer edge.

Triangle

WHEN HER FACE IS TRIANGULAR

Characteristics: Wide chin and narrow forehead
The Goal: Narrow the chin and widen the forehead

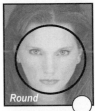

Round

Pick a style with full volume at the sides to balance her face shape. Style hair full at the temples, brushed away from the face and up toward the ear to widen the forehead. From the ear, angle hair forward toward the chin to soften and narrow a strong jaw. Chin length or longer hair will look best.

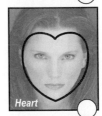

Heart

WHEN HER FACE IS ROUND

Characteristics: Wide, with full cheeks and a circular form
The Goal: Make face look slimmer; lengthen or narrow her features

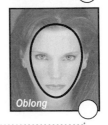

Oblong

Beautiful Hair—Knowing the Woman Who Seeks It

Find a style to help slim down the face. Below-the-chin styles should be styled with a face-lengthening center part. For above-the-chin styles, administer an off-center part. Keep a little height at the crown and slim the face by keeping her forehead uncluttered by bangs. In a short, angled style, keep hair away from the face, and add a little height at the crown to lengthen the look of her features. If she does want bangs, tousle them toward the side. Keep longer styles close to her face.

WHEN HER FACE IS HEART-SHAPED

Characteristics: Wide brow, full and prominent cheekbones and a narrow chin
The Goal: Narrow the forehead, widen the jaw line

Try reducing the width of her forehead by parting hair in the center and flipping bangs upward or styling hair slanted to one side with a side part. You can also help to make the lower part of her face look a little wider to balance out her proportions by styling her hair at shoulder length or turned under at the chin; mid-neck length will work best. Create fullness at the bottom and direct hair forward onto the cheeks, or try some curls or waves from the ears down.

WHEN HER FACE IS OBLONG

Characteristics: Long, thin face with a pointy chin
The Goal: Shorten things a bit

Try a low side part with a sweep of hair brushed diagonally across the forehead and gently combed in place. A voluminous look with an asymmetric hair flow to one side will create the illusion of width over length, as will straight bangs or bangs blended

with the sides of her hair. Mid-neck length will look best and styles
with curls, waves, and volume will look extremely flattering.

WHEN HER FACE IS DIAMOND-SHAPED

Characteristics: Narrow to near points at forehead and chin,
wider at cheeks
*The Goal: Fill in across the top and bottom to an extent so she can
really sparkle*

Framing is this girl's best friend: consider styles that keep hair
close to the head at the cheekbone line to create fullness across
the jaw and forehead. Styles that lift away from the cheeks or
move back from the hairline should be avoided.

WHEN HER FACE IS PEAR-SHAPED

Characteristics: Noticeably wider at the jaw than the forehead
The Goal: Balancing act

Hair should be styled fairly close to the top of her head with
a fringe of curls and bangs, combined with fullness at the sides
to make her forehead appear a little wider and to add balance.

Skin Tone: Watch Your Tone!

Your client may also want to choose a new hair color, or choose a
color for any replacement or additional hair you incorporate into
her repertoire. It's also helpful to choose a variety of colors, or at
least more than one, because varying shades subtly can help
mask new hair or divert attention from thinning and mild loss.

Before embarking on color selection, first determine whether
your client has warm or cool skin tones. A quick test we do in

front of a mirror works very well for our clients: throw colored scarves over her shoulders, preferably one at a time, and see which color is most pleasing to the eye (her eye is most important) at first glance. Start with blues and reds, as they are initially the most telling, and work from there.

Here's a basic guideline regarding skin tones to help you make a stronger assessment. For all initial evaluations, use your instincts about what looks right to the eye at first glance. Then take a long look with your client and see how you both feel about the color in conjunction with her overall appearance. Again, form your professional opinion, but realize that it is her preference that counts most. If colors are selected and she is wearing them and simply not feeling "herself," then her dissatisfaction will be unfortunate for you both. She must like what she sees.

Warm Skin Tones

If you lay a richly hued blue scarf around the front of her upper body, across from shoulder to shoulder, and it either is unpleasing to the eye or does nothing in particular for her, then try a red scarf of the same intensity. If the red scarf jives more with her overall appearance and makes your client feel good about how she looks, then you should consider her a person with warm skin tone. (The opposite holds true for the wearer of the blue scarf; she would have a cool skin tone.) For warm skin tones, brighten skin undertones by selecting hair colors with shades of reds, golds, and true browns. Avoid pale blondes and ashy shades. For pale yellow undertones, try light reds, golden blondes, and light browns. For golden yellow undertones, try medium reds and medium to light browns. For olive ash undertones, try medium auburns, medium reds, and dark browns.

Cool Skin Tones

If you drape a red fabric across your client's body and it does nothing for her or just doesn't look good for whatever reason, and then you try the blue and it's a whole other story, she is a person with a cool skin tone. Warm and soften skin undertones with natural hair shades of ash, honey, and chestnut. Avoid strong reddish shades.

Take a good look to see what undertone tendencies your client possesses. For pale pink undertones, try light ash blonde, light brown, honey blonde, and the lightest browns. For rose undertones, try medium blonde, and light and medium browns. For reddish blue undertones, try ash blonde, dark ash blond, and dark brown.

One of the most important concepts to adhere to when making your color decisions is to stay away from overshadowing your client's features. Color should enhance, not overpower, her natural beauty.

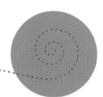

THE PERSONAL PROFILE

Lifestyle Q & A

After you evaluate your client's face shape and some of the flattering styles to go with it, you should ask her questions about her hair, her personality, and her lifestyle. Her answers—combined with the face-shape styling options selected—will help you and your client decide about her new hairstyle, and will also help determine which other solutions might work for her. These answers may also determine the need for other kinds of experts to help her with other aspects of her hair loss.

Ask these questions of your clients when they first come in for a consultation. The questions are important in beginning the process of finding solutions, and they should be addressed before the first styling step is taken:

- Are you inactive or extremely active?
- Do you chemically process your hair?
- What concerns you most about your hair at this time?
- Which aspects of your hair would you like to enhance (e.g., texture, volume, color, wave, length)?
- Is your hair fine or thin?
- Do you find that most styling products weigh down your hair?
- Are you noticing more hair on your pillow, in the shower drain, or on your hairbrush?
- Have any of your family members experienced hair thinning or hair loss? If so, who?
- Have you found that hair on top of your head grows in shorter than the rest of your hair?
- Have you experienced irritation of the scalp?
- Are you undergoing any medical treatment? If so, what type?
- Have you already experienced hair loss? If yes, for how long?

You may go into greater detail during consultation to find out more about how a client's hair styling and hair care regimen will have to fit into her lifestyle. Ask:

- Do you spend a lot of time at the beach, in a pool, on a motorcycle, or in constantly windy conditions? Do you spend your days climbing telephone poles for a living or chasing your two-year-old child through the neighborhood tot lot?

- Are you constantly in the public eye, on television or in court, or do you rebind old books in the local library's antiquated sciences section? Which activities are you most often involved in and in what kind of environments and climates (both at work and socially)? What kind of appearance do you need to convey to your coworkers, superiors, clients, and the public?
- Do you spend hours getting ready for the day or are you a no-nonsense, five-minute-morning person?
- Are you naturally good at dealing with your hair or do you feel you were never particularly good at styling it?
- How would you categorize your hair texture?
- Do you have a natural and persistent part?
- Does your hair ever get extremely oily or dry?
- Are you more comfortable with long or short styles? Does the shape or length of your body, or the slant of your ears, or the interesting-to-everyone-else-but-you scar over your eye have anything to do with what you are looking for in a hairstyle?

All of the answers to the above questions are pertinent to your client's total approach to strategically treating and styling her hair. The information revealed by her honest answers may play a role in other solutions she seeks in the future, beyond hair styling and framing.

Pull Test

In addition to the Diffusion Grade and Pattern Stage indicators described at the end of the previous chapter, a helpful indicator of your client's degree of hair thinning and loss lies in what's called a "pull test."

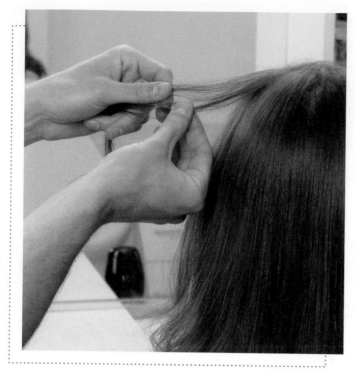

Draw on your client's hair (after describing what you will be doing and why). To "draw on" means to pull moderately, closer to lightly than hard, in five to eight different locations on her head. If one hair comes out in five pulls, it's normal. If hair comes out 50 percent of the time, it's a problem. This will help you assess if your client will need to have a doctor's input or evaluation.

With test results and information from the hair loss history/health assessment, a good health professional can usually pinpoint the causes of your client's hair loss, and recommend solutions that are available to help you solve her hair loss problem. It would be helpful to you as the hair restoration and replacement specialist if your client were to share that information with you, at her discretion. You can work without that information and be successful, but it helps to have all the information about her circumstances that she is willing to convey.

But if specific causes can't be identified even after all the research is signed, sealed, and delivered, it shouldn't keep your client from beginning to address the problem and work on applying solutions. There are enough ways to handle hair loss to enable her to start treating the symptoms, while you help her regain her natural beauty and self-esteem.

CONSULTATION TOOL LIST

The following list will help you prepare for and conduct your client profile and consultation:

color selection chart	extension strand-by-strand and lineal combination	cutting shears
material guide and hair sample comparisons	client profile	fine point black marker
density guide	before and after portfolio	grease pencil
highlight-lowlight guide	tape measure	four to six hair clips
grey percentage guide	appropriate color ring for design	hair style book or flip chart of before and afters
wave texture guide	blending shears	hand mirror
demo half-head design series model	brush	Polaroid camera with film
integration design	calculator	six-inch ruler
duplication design	clipboard	tape in tape dispenser
full head pre-custom design	comb	pre-consultation video
full head custom design	colored highlighters	VCR with monitor
		video rewinder

In the next chapter we will take a look at some of the solutions you can apply for hair thinning and hair loss.

Beautiful Hair—Knowing the Woman Who Seeks It

BEAUTIFUL REPLACEMENT HAIR—
What It's All About

*Components of Restoring
Beautiful Hair*

CHAPTER

4

INTRODUCTION

Let's take a look at the kinds of hair we use in creating hair replacements, and the aspects of replacement that you should be aiming to fulfill in devising the best and most natural effect in your final product. This section will describe the kinds of replacement hair and how they are processed and prepared, as well as types of replacements available and what they serve to recreate. It's amazing that cosmetic therapists are able to turn human and synthetic hair into beautiful, natural-looking hair that is easy to maintain and complements a woman's lifestyle. By recreating or enhancing the five characteristics of beautiful, natural, growing hair in replacement hair, we are able to achieve this phenomenon.

The main goal in restoring the look of the original hair is to replenish the five main characteristics of the client's hair that made it attractive. By replenishing those characteristics, you can give the illusion of naturally beautiful hair once again. You can even incorporate some characteristics she wishes her natural hair had had, but that depends on how true to her original look she wants to remain.

Shine is a given with good quality hair. To insure that shine and luster endure for the life of the replacement hair, it's important to maintain the hair, both at home and in the salon, with the proper shampoo, protein treatment, and conditioners.

Different conditioners do different things for different types of hair, and it would help if you had an idea of which to recommend for your client's specific hair type. Protein conditioners boost shine, improve body, and extend the life of the replacement hair. Moisture and detangling conditioners help restore moisture balance to treated and processed hair. Spray conditioners, used on a daily basis, help keep the replacement hair manageable and help maintain its proper moisture levels.

Hair *color* is a very individual characteristic. To create vibrantly colored hair, we do what Mother Nature would have intended. Using replacement hair that is natural, synthetic, or a mix of the two, we blend different colored strands together with a brushlike tool called a hackle in order to create the desired color. If we can't get the shade and the corresponding highlights we want by blending available hair, we can also use dyes and bleaches.

Texture is something you see and feel, and whether it's a slight wave in fine hair or a tight curl in coarse hair, you can replicate it in replacement hair. Sometimes the visual and tactile character of natural hair can be created with strand extensions, which are bonded to existing hair to increase volume and length. At other times it can be created with integration "systems" (fabric that has new hair attached to it with strategic openings for your client's own hair to come through) to add volume, density, length, and color. When full coverage is the goal, the hair in a custom-designed hair replacement can either be permed or styled for desired weight and pattern, or it can be textured during processing to replicate specific ethnic qualities.

Growth is both the easiest and hardest of the five characteristics of healthy, natural hair to duplicate. The ease is due to the ability to choose the length. The difficulty is that replacement hair won't actually look like it's growing. But with replacement hair, you can give the illusion of healthy hair, which everyone assumes is growing beautifully.

Framing the face with hair in a new way can also minimize the appearance of loss or thinning. Every individual face is unique because of things like eye shape, chin length, lip width, and a variety of other characteristics. That means that to create what is truly the right frame, replacement hair must be individually cut and styled. So whether it's a tiny addition at the top of the head or a custom-designed full medical prosthesis (custom wig), it needs to be designed and styled to complement your client's special qualities and overall appearance. Styling is both an art and a science that brings out her best features, minimizes her least favorite ones, and even has the power to complement her body shape and physical build.

MATERIALS AND METHODS

The following will briefly tell you about the three kinds of replacement hair. Some of the sources may seem odd, but most people would never guess where the hair comes from and would never guess that it is not natural.

Fiber Comparison Chart

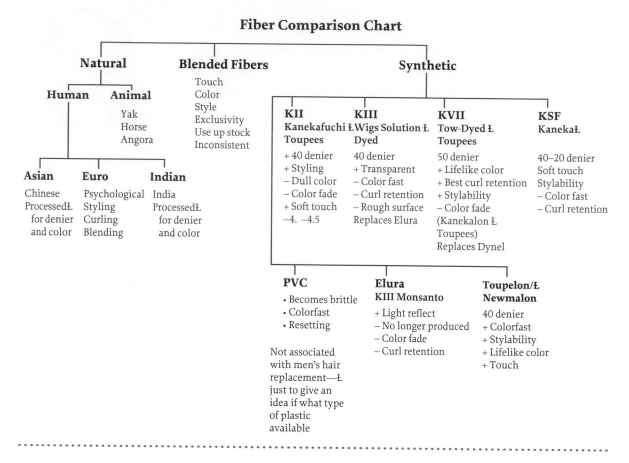

Natural   **Blended Fibers**   **Synthetic**

Human   **Animal**

Blended Fibers:
Touch
Color
Style
Exclusivity
Use up stock
Inconsistent

Animal:
Yak
Horse
Angora

Asian   **Euro**   **Indian**

Asian:
Chinese
ProcessedŁ
for denier
and color

Euro:
Psychological
Styling
Curling
Blending

Indian:
India
ProcessedŁ
for denier
and color

KII
Kanekafuchi Ł
Toupees

+ 40 denier
+ Styling
– Dull color
– Color fade
+ Soft touch
–4. –4.5

KIII
Wigs Solution Ł
Dyed

40 denier
+ Transparent
– Color fast
– Curl retention
– Rough surface
Replaces Elura

KVII
Tow-Dyed Ł
Toupees

50 denier
+ Lifelike color
+ Best curl retention
+ Stylability
– Color fade
(Kanekalon Ł
Toupees)
Replaces Dynel

KSF
KanekaŁ

40–20 denier
Soft touch
Stylability
– Color fast
– Curl retention

PVC

• Becomes brittle
• Colorfast
• Resetting

Not associated
with men's hair
replacement—Ł
just to give an
idea if what type
of plastic
available

Elura
KIII Monsanto

+ Light reflect
– No longer produced
– Color fade
– Curl retention

**Toupelon/Ł
Newmalon**

40 denier
+ Colorfast
+ Stylability
+ Lifelike color
+ Touch

The most popular, and least expensive, kind of replacement hair is synthetic hair. Mimicking fine, medium, or coarse hair and giving a soft and silky feel, most synthetic hair is made of polyester, polyvinyl chloride (PVC), or modacrylic fiber (such as Kanekalon, which is used in 75 percent of all synthetic wigs and hairpieces). All come in a wide array of colors for your client's needs, and all are easy to "program." In other words, the hair stays true to styling and restyling efforts.

"Pieces are curled in an oven at 212 degrees Fahrenheit for one hour," says Charlotte Jayne, co-founder and executive vice president of Garland Drake International, a major supplier of natural human hair. PVC is more suitable for long and wavy styles and modacrylic is more suitable for short and curly ones. Today, most synthetic hair goods are a blend of both in a ratio that best suits particular styles.

What the Different Materials Mean to You

Synthetic

Darla Smith, vice president of Technical Services at International Hair Goods, says that synthetic hair (man-made hair) doesn't fade as quickly or lose its wave as fast as human hair does, and that it's stronger. However, if it's not made properly, it can look artificial. Synthetic hair includes materials like nylon, Cyberhair, monocrylic, Polyvinylchloride (PVC), and polyester.

Monocrylic and Polyvinylchloride (PVC) replacement hair are both easy to maintain, so hair additions or wigs created with that type of hair will require less energy and time on your client's part. They are also lighter in weight than human hair. Polyester and nylon will hold their wave to the end of time, and color also attaches well to nylon. Polyester hair has more longevity than monocrylic, but not as much nylon. Nylon and Cyberhair are the most expensive, with polyester, monocrylic, and PVC following in that order. Nylon is the most expensive (it can be up to five times more expensive than PVC) due to colorfastness, stability, light weight, and ability to maintain curl and reflect light. Nylon is not your option for length or integration of growing hair. Human hair is best for that.

There are some basic advantages and disadvantages to synthetic hair that are important to understand.

PRO:

does not fade

does not lose curl pattern

lightweight

sheds less

comes in a variety of styles

CON:

cannot change color

does not reflect sunlight (can begin to look dull)

may be affected by heat and cold

can be difficult to blend with existing hair

tangles easily if used in strands longer than 10 inches

Natural

Two other kinds of replacement hair come from natural sources. They are human hair and animal hair. Animal hair can originate from—of all places—the underbellies of yaks, horses' tails, and the backs of angora rabbits. It retains the outer cuticle, which protects the hair shaft and gives it its shine and resilience. Human hair used for replacement comes from three geographic areas—Europe (mostly the countries of the former Soviet Union), China, and India—and it comes in several grades.

European hair—often marketed as "genuine European hair"—commands top dollar. One of the reasons is that the diameter of the hair is closest to the diameter of Caucasian hair, whose wearers are demanding the product. But the cost of it is very much related to the difficulty in obtaining it. Because it is not as common for European women in certain countries to indulge in visits to a salon (as it is for their Western counterparts), the hair is virtually untreated, unprocessed, and is considered "virgin" hair. "Virgin" hair is the most stable and the highest quality hair available.

Chinese hair is darker, straighter, and coarser—due to the thicker hair shaft—than European hair and there is a lot of it available. To turn it into usable hair, however, it has to be stripped of most of its outer cuticle layer. This, unfortunately, makes the hair shaft thinner, dryer, and more brittle. To restore the hair's resilience and sheen, it must be coated with silicone. The silicone isn't permanent. It washes off the hair shafts after a few shampoos.

The best all-around hair available today is Indian hair. Indian hair has a slight wave to it and, because of genetic similarities, it's very similar in both color and hair shaft diameter to various types of Caucasian hair. Also, when it is treated correctly in processing, it brings about the most accommodating attributes, and is closest to some Caucasian hair in terms of shine and texture, and is durable and easy to care for.

Most important, it is collected using the best method possible. Most traditional Indian women cut off their long hair for special occasions, such as a wedding, the birth of a child, or even to ask a favor of or offer thanks to a deity. The hair, in tight braids with all the hairs (and hair cuticles) aligned in one direction—which makes it easier to work with—is then collected by hair merchants, most of whom are from Korea or Indonesia.

Isaac Bracha is the owner and president of Hair and

Beautiful Replacement Hair—What It's All About

Compounds in Los Angeles. It operates the only research and development laboratory for replacement hair, and the India-based Different Hair, which processes human hair from its raw state for use in replacement. Bracha explains why human hair is so popular.

"Human hair does not look fake because we are able to recreate the color and the texture for the most perfect match," he says. "When clients order hair through their specialist, a micrometer is ultimately used to measure the diameter of their hair, and we search out hair that has equal or similar diameter." According to Bracha, that's the first step in matching hair well to its consumer, since replacement hair will best mimic its wearer's hair if it is extremely close in diameter. Diameter affects the weight of the hair, the way it falls, and other important factors that will become obvious if there is a large discrepancy.

There are also advantages and disadvantages to using natural replacement hair.

PRO:

can be treated/maintained like your own hair

has excellent color blend ability/flexibility

has good movement, body, stylability

can be permed and retexturized

CON:

can be expensive

can be slightly heavier than synthetic

can shed faster than synthetic

has limited variety

It's important that you deal with a reputable company in ordering replacement hair. According to Bracha, smaller companies may have hair lab operations that allow for more personal involvement, while major manufacturers may operate on more of an assembly line basis. If you have any questions regarding outcome after ordering hair of certain color, texture, and other characteristics, you can request what is called a "hair approval" so that a small sample can be sent in advance for you to examine.

Readying the Hair for Use

Bracha further asserts that smaller companies differ greatly from major manufacturing companies in how hair is prepared for use. Smaller "boutique" operations may employ a higher level of quality control. For example, smaller companies may seek the finest hair because they have a more personalized operation, whereas larger manufacturers operating on more of an assembly line basis may not get the best quality in every case.

Bracha explains that the basic process of preparing hair is as follows: The hair comes to the company in raw bundles. Very short hairs (two to three inch strands) are discarded since they can't be used. The hair is then divided into small bundles so that whatever chemicals and conditioners are used in the processing can penetrate the hair fully. You can't, after all, just pour some solution onto a batch of hair and expect that it will reach the innermost core of hair. (In some places, like Asia, that is actually done, and then hair is laid outside on concrete in the parking lot to dry.) Hair is then shampooed and conditioned thoroughly. Shampooing allows for detergent to clean the surface of unwanted particles and possible bacteria (although bacteria is not commonly found on the hair). A special shampoo is used to keep hair from becoming dry. It was selected with the same attention one would use in selecting a gentle soap to avoid allergic reactions or rashes while being effective enough to cleanse well.

The conditioner that is used is intended to reduce friction between two fibers (think of a fabric softener that keeps socks from sticking together in the dryer). According to Bracha, aside from chemical interference, the greatest damage done to hair is from combing it right away when it's wet. It is important to work hair in one direction, dividing hair into manageable sections and gently pressing it to blot out wetness. These instructions are for the wearer at home as well. Remembering how the replacement hair was so carefully handled will provide a basis for client maintenance at home, so feel free to share your knowledge on the subject.

Take It Off! Cuticle and Non-Cuticle

Bracha says that removing cuticle will keep replacement hair from tangling, but since the hair's cuticle acts as protection for the hair (like our skin, which protects the vulnerable tissues beneath it), there are consequences that limit the overall life of the product. "Without its cuticle, the strength and elasticity of replacement hair is reduced by about 25 percent," says Bracha. "The moisture of the hair can usually be measured at around 10–10.5 percent of the hair's composition, depending upon the climate of the environment it came from. If it's a more humid environment, there will be more moisture present in the hair. Once we remove the hair's cuticle—which is necessary more than 95 percent of the time in order for it to be used for replacement purposes—the moisture decreases. This is largely because we have to take chemical action to remove the cuticle. This draws out the moisture."

Some hair still has its cuticle. This is called *remy/cuticle* hair. With this type, roots must be kept aligned in one direction and the returns must be trimmed short. This type is healthy hair with the most natural appearance—basically, virgin hair—and thus it must be tied in this particular way to avoid tangling.

Two other kinds of hair emerge from the preparation process, both of which have had some degree of cuticle removal. *Remy/non-cuticle* is one kind. With this type of hair, it is not necessary to keep roots in one direction as tangling isn't likely. The outer cuticle layer has been chemically processed which decreases the hair's natural health and shine. This type of replacement hair is best because it is practical, it is not sensitive to various conditions, it can be swum in and slept in, and it is durable and easy to care for.

The other kind is called *non-remy/non-cuticle;* it has undergone complete cuticle removal. With this type of hair, it is not necessary to keep the roots aligned in one direction. Bundles do not contain shorter lengths of hair. The hair has been processed with chemicals that cause additional damage. It is more prone to split ends, color fading, and slight tangling on the ends. After three months, the differences between remy and non-remy become more obvious. Because all of the cuticle has been removed, this hair is the least expensive.

Under Constant Surveillance

Hair has to undergo a bleaching process in order to accept its new color, especially since so much of the human replacement hair is originally very dark. Hair is shampooed and conditioned continually in order to overcome the problem of reduced moisture. After all, most hair no longer has cuticle to prevent it from drying out. Conditioning also deposits temporary strength into the hair, so you need to repeat the process while waiting for the hair to be shipped.

Pretty Hair Processing: Not a Pretty Process

Before human hair can be turned into a hairpiece or wig, it has to be processed. First the hair is "bathed" in a bath of muriatic acid and scrubbed to remove most of the outer cuticle. "Removing the cuticle is a tricky process," says Garland Drake International's Charlotte Jayne. "Removing too little of the hair shaft's protective layer will leave the hair prone to matting and tangling. Removing too much will leave it prone to breakage and prevent it from taking on colorants or dyes."

Then hair is "rinsed" in a chemical solution (to neutralize the acid) and "de-colorized" (a fancy way of saying it's bleached) to remove the hair's natural color. As bleaching can take up to 15 days and requires a precise mix of chemicals, water, and heat, it is best if the process is overseen by a chemist.

Then it's "texturized"—waved, curled, or crimped by wrapping it around wooden rods of various widths in another chemical bath. Then it's dyed, using chrome dyes, the same kind used

Bracha states that some communities, such as the orthodox Jewish community, request that the initial portion of the V be cut so as not to interfere with the returns. This is a costlier process, but it can be done. It is requested roughly five percent of the time.

to color the wool for carpets and rugs. "Usually," says Jayne, "dyed hair is not marked as dyed hair, whereas hair that is not dyed usually is marked as non-dyed hair."

And finally, the hair is prepared for sale. Hair that will be used for wigs and hairpieces is sold as bulk hair; hair that will be used for extensions is sold as a weft—a strong, thin thread that has individual hairs tied or machine-sewn to it.

The Point of Return and the Point of No Return

When replacement hair systems are created, they need ventilation. Hair is tied into systems in much the same manner as carpets are woven, or as hook-rugs are constructed. Each hair is folded like a "V," the point of which is the point of connection to the system in a tiny knot (this is not true in certain types of extensions; consult Chapter 5). The second part of the V shape comes back as the hair seen with your client's own and is called "the return." Because of the positioning of the hair in a V shape, hair cuticles on both sides of the V will be running in opposite directions. When you look at cuticle under a microscope, you can see that it is made up of small twig-like "limbs" that stick out. When those limbs run in the same direction, hair is smooth and untangled. When the replacement hair is tied into a V shape, both the initial end and the return end of the V have cuticle limbs that will rub against one another and cause tangling and matting.

Technological Breakthrough

Knowing how detrimental it is to remove cuticle, Bracha experimented and came up with a type of chemical that would stick to replacement hair, but would not cause damage to the hair or weigh it down. He wanted to make sure that it wouldn't change the color, shine, or flexibility of the hair, which ultimately defines the body and movement of hair. This chemical covers the cuticle and flattens it so that it won't tangle on the return. The name of this chemical is CNC, which stands for cuticle non-cuticle, and it enables the manufacturer to take cuticled hair and keep the cuticle on, but have the hair behave like decuticled hair. Hair and Compounds is the originator of this special technology, and Bracha estimates that it will cost roughly 25–35 percent more because of the tedious technique and added work involved in processing.

Color It Beautiful

According to Smith of International Hair Goods, when hair is stripped of its cuticle, it not only becomes more fragile, it also will lose its color faster. But the process is necessary to keep hair from matting and tangling. "Replacement hair's color should last approximately three months after processing, and about five months if it's unprocessed," says Smith. Replacement hair systems can be colored to be refreshed, but extensions are temporary and should be replaced.

The color of replacement hair can be customized using a number of methods to create the best imitation of your client's natural hair, Smith says. It can be highlighted by mixing shades of blonde and brown together, adding a third color for more of an effect, or creating standard highlights that are evenly blended. Manufacturers can do a partial mix, which entails some streaking and rougher blending for better color effects. You can get or create replacement hair that has been sun-streaked or foiled, with light and dark squares or sections interspersed throughout. Marbleized replacement hair is also an option, which involves triple streaking (interspersing light, medium, and dark sections). You can also shoot for spotlighted replacement hair for that unusual birthmark effect. Finally, Smith says that yak belly hair is the best option for gray hair replacements.

HAIR SHOPPING

Since you will be the one ordering the hair for your client after the important decisions have been made, you should know something about quality and how to assess it. Different *quality* hair is used in hair replacement. Good quality is important, and the quality of human hair has many variables. A local supply store may sell human hair inexpensively, while some manufacturers sell grades of human hair for hefty prices. You may find that, with more expensive human hair, the price is often a good indicator of better quality. It's always good to make sure the manufacturer or hair lab is reputable before buying there. The varied quality, processing, and origins of the hair account for price differences.

According to Smith, it will take a week of "wear" to see the hair's real character and quality. The reason for this is that manufacturers coat hair with silicone, but after a few washes the hair will begin to exhibit characteristics that were hidden by the silicone when your client purchased it. After you have been through hair selection many times and know the best companies to buy from, you will get a knack for what to select. But meanwhile, your client will look to you to help find various characteristics in replacement hair, such as the right hair texture. There's everything from straight to kinky to chemically processed or straightened hair. Choosing length and color is important, but texture is the most important factor; volume should be determined along with your texture choice.

The Kinds of Hair Replacements

In the next chapter, you will find out everything you need to know about hair replacement options. We'll start with extensions, integrations, and duplication systems, and move on to wigs, full cranial prosthetics, and hair additions and alternatives. Briefly, different kinds of attachment methods and materials provide your client with choices about how long to wear her hair replacement. For daily wear replacements, attachment methods range from combs, clips, and clamps to elastic bands, hats, and head coverings that may have replacement hair attached to them. For extended wear replacements, attachment methods range from the more stressful sewing, braiding, and weaving, to the more common medical adhesives and cold or hot bonds, and even vacuum pressure placement. Some replacements come with adhesives and some do not. Some allow you to use special linking techniques or to use your client's own hair to hold them in place. There are many possibilities, depending on the type of replacement selected and what your client's needs are. We will look more closely at these details in the next chapter as we describe different solutions.

Turnaround Time

There are five ways hair replacements are manufactured or designed, and the one you choose will determine how quickly you get your hair replacement:

Ready-made (machine-made): When you order your hair replacement from stock, the selection available to you is what the manufacturer has in stock. You can choose the style and color, order it, and get it right away, but the design and construction will be determined by what's in stock and that's it. There are one or two sizes that "fit all."

Pre-custom (hand-tied): With these hair replacements, you can choose from the manufacturer's inventory, which is a selected inventory of hand-tied replacements. The manufacturer decides on design and construction, but you can make your selection and get it right away. Sizes are small, medium, and large.

Semi-custom (hand-tied from cap system, or duplication of pre-custom to specialized needs): When you order these replacements, you can select from categories and have them customized based on your client's needs. You can get these within four to six weeks of ordering. Size is determined from six to eight specific measurements of the head.

Full custom (hand-tied from mold): Hair replacements in this category are individualized. You decide what design and materials you'd like, and how you want it to be constructed. You can expect to have it within six to ten weeks.

In-house custom: In this case, you work with your client to design exactly what she needs. You place caps with different design capabilities over her head, or take measurements to design and fabricate the cap with her individual concerns in mind, and then you order the appropriate materials and construct it on your premises. This process takes about eight to twelve weeks. This method does not employ state of the art technology in processing the final product, and is an old-world and theatrical practice that can produce hair replacement on site. Professionals who develop skills for this option often specialize in such targeted customization for different industries, for example, theatrical or screen entertainment outlets.

The Base of the Replacement

You will be responsible for knowing all there is to know about replacement materials, and you should be aware of what materials are typically used to create the base of a replacement and what their general properties are. Two categories of materials are used in constructing hair replacement systems (extensions do not apply here, and neither do most hair additions and alternatives). Fabrics, such as polyester and nylon, are available in varying degrees of thickness and weave. Polyester is opaque, strong, and easy to fix if it needs fixing. Nylon is usually transparent and can be colored to match your client's scalp. It is heat-formed to follow the contours of her scalp from the molds that are taken during her custom design. Polymers, such as polyurethane and silicone, are used where scalp and skin likeness is desired. Polyurethane looks most like skin, and is flexible and easy to attach. Silicone is soft, stretchy, and looks a lot like skin, but it is harder to attach than polyurethane. Silicone will last longer than other polymers when exposed to the chemicals used on the replacement hair that's attached to it.

BEAUTIFUL HAIR—
How to Give It Back

Hair Restoration and Replacement Solutions

CHAPTER 5

INTRODUCTION

Solutions for women's hair thinning and hair loss include options ranging from non-invasive preventive treatments and camouflage makeup to hair replacement and surgery. In this chapter you will find detailed guidance on how to offer your clients 10 solutions that may work for them depending upon their pattern stages, diffusion grades, lifestyles, preferences, and needs:

- styling and framing techniques, specifically for thin hair
- camouflage makeup—colored creams and pressed powders to conceal areas where hair is thinning
- topical and nutritional hair care treatments that can be applied or employed to nourish and strengthen the hair, and laser-light therapy to accelerate the effects of treatments by drawing nourishment from the blood to the scalp
- hair extensions, through which length, fullness, and texture are added to natural hair via strand-by-strand and lineal bonding
- hair integration, where a small hair system combines with natural growing hair to fill in areas
- hair duplication, designed for more extensive coverage to restore the appearance of a full head of hair
- wigs and full cranial prosthetics—a complete, full-head prosthesis designed for women with extreme hair loss
- hair alternatives, which provide fashionable accessories covering the head, with new hair attached to them as an option
- hair additions, which are fashionable accessories that are made out of "new" hair and that can be worn with hair to simulate fullness and growth

- surgical hair restoration, through which micro- and mini-grafts are attached to the scalp for permanent restoration of growing hair

If you didn't already know it, you can now see that there is a list of solutions that have worked beautifully for women seeking to restore or replace their hair. Few women are aware of these potential solutions, and that is why their situation remains dire to them. When they find out what you know, they will be instantly relieved of some of their concern and fear. Then, you are not only providing them with a real solution to their predicament, you are also helping them to feel better and live more positively again, which is the real gift this opportunity bestows upon you.

Many clients will come to you when their hair has thinned so much that they can no longer hide their problem, no matter how hard they try. They will tell you that you are their last resort. Respond by saying that talking with you is only one of a series of options. They will ask, "What can I do?" You can answer, "What can't you do."

The solutions presented in this book cover a range from the early stages of thinning or loss of hair, when people start looking for a style to hide their problem, to later stages, when people realize other treatments might work better for their advanced needs. For example, if your client just realized that her hair thinning has become noticeable, you might advise her to try some preventative measures and then apply camouflage makeup or restyle and color her hair. On the other hand, if she has more progressive hair loss, she might stop using camouflage makeup and opt for integrating hair or doing something more permanent. A lot depends on how progressive her condition is and what kind of lifestyle she leads.

Ideally, the hair loss remedy your client selects will be based on a combination of what's best for her circumstances, and what she feels she can put into the effort. This program could be one or a combination of these outlined solutions, which make up a total approach to the hair thinning or hair loss problem.

Now let's take a look at the top 10 categories of solutions we've found to be the most effective for clients at various stages of their hair loss. When you're finished learning the basics of what these solutions entail, and how to administer them, you'll be well versed for detailed consultations with your clients, and you'll be able to offer them many of these solutions on your own.

STYLING AND FRAMING— The First Fast Fix

The fastest and most obvious solution for your clients who are ready to treat their hair loss is to change their hairstyle. Styling is the tool that can be used immediately to begin the process of looking better, even while clients are continuing to explore other treatments. It's the first thing people notice and the fastest way to divert attention away from the issue. What's more, the hairstyle you and your client choose is not set in stone. As time goes by and you try other solutions, she may choose to change her style again.

In order to choose the right style, it's important to evaluate the shape of her face and analyze how much hair she has per square inch of her scalp. Next, you should consider whether hair will need perming or coloring to assist in good styling. This evaluation process is a unique approach, but is necessary. Here's why: Let's say your client walks into a regular hair salon. The stylist will most likely take one look at her hair and chop into it, since most stylists respond to thinning hair by seriously layering to make hair appear fuller. Often, especially with women who have fine hair, this leads to a "shredded wheat" effect. There's no buoyancy or density to hair after this fiasco.

Specialists like you, on the other hand, belong to a kinder and gentler styling nation. You know you can turn hair into a silky bob, an elegant and shiny chignon, or any number of other successful styles from first glance. In fact, you welcome the

MOST IDEAL FOR:
early stages of hair thinning and loss, but good to know for all clients

challenge because you are trained to be sensitive to your clients' needs.

We've all heard stories about—or worked with—hairdressers who become offended when a woman comes to them with photographs or with a definite idea of what she wants. Yet women have a sense of the look they know works best for their silhouette and frame. The nature of a woman is to know this, even when she doesn't realize it. For example, even if she's not sure what works, she inherently knows what doesn't. She responds to what would look good on her when she sees it on

CHAPTER 5

someone else, or if she has seen it on herself. When she tries to convey it to a stylist, that stylist should do his or her best to really hear what she is saying, because that will mean she'll leave truly satisfied.

As you are listening carefully to what your client's thoughts and needs are, you will evaluate the shape of her face to determine how to frame her hair around it in the most flattering way. This is really important, because it affects her entire image and helps to detract attention from any potential hair issues.

Think about where Jennifer Aniston would be if she didn't sport the face-framing tendrils on *Friends*. Would Marilyn Monroe have gone as far with Norma Jean's hairstyle? We know very well the effect styling and framing has and it's exciting to think of what good-looking changes may be in store for your clients—and what new developments may be in store for you professionally—as they begin to deal with their hair loss issues.

Three women are shown on the next two pages to help illustrate styling and framing solutions that show how examining lifestyle and hair needs can lead to a knockout style. One is an example of short hair, another of medium-length hair, and the last of long hair. Each woman had her hair styled with her face shape, daily routine, and personality all taken into consideration, and the resulting looks made a big difference in each of their lives.

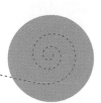

YOUR PROFESSIONAL RESPONSIBILITY:
What to Tell Women About Finding the Right Stylist

Women know that it is possible to find products and stylists separately, but it is better to find a stylist they can trust to recommend

Student Is No Square

Age: Thirties

Michelle has a square-shaped face, thin hair, and a long neck. Her hair will fluff and look like it has more volume, but not after it surpasses three or four inches in length. We framed her square face by styling a soft fringe of hair around it, which makes it look more oval. We gave her peek-a-boo bangs and layered her hair longer around her neck. The overall effect is softer, with greater volume and a style that is kicky and fun—perfect for her lifestyle as a college student on the go.

Professional with Versatile Portfolio

Age: Forties

Ann has a sophisticated position at work. She also has a long, triangular face. Layering her hair into a short style would be the wrong look for her and would also show too much of her scalp. Instead, we created a bob for her at the longest length at which her hair can hold its true strength, and then we added a few long layers for a little lift and more stability. We also trained her in specific styling techniques, which are basically more diffusion-oriented than heat-dependent, since hair shrinks and gets tighter under heat conditions. The result is a chin-length bob. We could also give her soft bangs, if she feels she can carry them, or simply part her hair on one side. With her new style, Ann can also tuck a side section of her hair behind her ear or create a little stacking to accentuate her cheekbones. The framing is there, but the style is soft enough to allow her to make subtle changes that can transform her look.

Long, Lovely, Lifted Layers

Age: Fifties

Sara is a great example of how we can give a woman security and coverage through her hairstyle. A lot of women are afraid that cutting their hair will make them look bald or more at risk. Some women experience thinning and loss, but say their husbands like them best with long hair, or that they feel younger with long hair. For these women, lifting their hair into a chignon or a twist while framing the face correctly will allow them to keep their hair long while venturing out into other attractive options. This style is cut to give Sara the ability to change and not necessarily lose hair length in the process. Thin hair can be worked with in this fashion and the length can be kept. For Sara, with her more rounded face, if her hair were worn straight down with little or no style, it would overframe her neck and the result would be a kind of lollipop look. So we put some soft layers on top and pulled the hair back to give it style, all the while framing the face. This also takes some weight off the top.

the right products for their particular circumstances. Your clients might start with a dermatologist, or go to a reputable treatment center where stylists have been trained in assessment, consultation, and developing strategies, such as a hair restoration or replacement center.

Advise women to try to find a stylist who will work with their hair in different angles as he or she styles, so as to determine how hair will fall under various conditions. Women are often afraid to change their style because they are afraid of what they might uncover or show to the world. It is important to try to style their hair so that when they make a few changes they don't even have to think about what may appear underneath. After all, a woman can't just stand around looking gorgeous all day. Style her thinning hair in a way that will give her back her lifestyle so that she doesn't have to worry about whether her hair will move and reveal the thinning areas. Too often, women with this challenge become dormant because it completely inhibits them. This fear, while understandable, should be rendered unnecessary.

You may also tell women that it's important to find stylists who really know their stuff. For example, many stylists are attached to the notion that you can't use a razor on very thin hair. It's not so; many specialty stylists know it's one of the most important tools for people with hair thinning and loss issues. You can use a razor a lot of the time to give thin hair blunt ends, and to do special cutting at the nape line or in upper areas to create more body.

A good haircut is also important for good styling. It is imperative that you listen well and not be limited in your ability to consider all options, all factors that contribute to your client's lifestyle, and the needs of your client's condition. Yet it's true that it also helps if you can deliver a great haircut!

Tell women not to commit to a stylist who immediately suggests all-over layering, coloring, or perming. Tell them to beware of this "band-aid on a deep wound" approach, which sometimes spells further hair loss. See if you can come up with a creative way of looking at your client's physical attributes and finding a complementary hairstyle that works with her lifestyle and looks.

Finally, tell women to try to find a stylist associated with a line of products designed specifically for thinning and loss issues, rather than a line of generalized or mainstream products.

Tell them to go for the counselor/artist over the salesperson. And when you make any product recommendations, such as sprays and other volumizing products to make hair look thicker, make sure they are gentle products designed for your client's problem.

The woman who turns to you for guidance regarding her hair loss concerns will also see you as her trainer—the one who answers the what and how of techniques, products, and other lifestyle tips that have an impact on her situation and its improvement. She will count on you to give her the right maintenance and at-home direction, and to find the answers if you do not know them from your own personal experience. Most of all, she will rely on your careful thinking with her situation in mind, and will drop you if you seem too casual about her problem, or if you give an answer you are not sure about. Be informed and genuine in order to gain your client's trust, and to develop with her the best final product for her circumstances. You are on this mission together and depend on each other for it to work out satisfactorily.

Clients will need to have their hair cut and use the proper products recommended to them during their consultation and service. It's also important that they are told:

1. It will take three to four cuts for them to discover their optimal design or style.

2. Products need 90 days of "test-driving" before changing them.

3. Thinning and slow-growing hair needs frequent cutting and servicing to grow at its ideal rate.

Beautiful Hair—How to Give It Back

TIPS FOR GREAT STYLING SUCCESS

There are different styling tools and practices that will help your clients protect the health of their existing hair and prevent further damage as they maintain their new style. Many women use combs to tease their hair to give it height at the crown of the head or volume on the sides. Teasing is a technique that was used a lot in the 1950s, but women who seek volume still resort to it. The biggest mistake women make when combing their hair is to use a narrow-tooth comb to detangle their wet hair. You and your clients should use wide-tooth combs, long-width combs that have soft, round-edged teeth that massage rather than irritate the scalp, or specialized brushes designed to flow through wet, thin hair or hair extensions without breaking the hair.

Too Hot To Handle

Some of the best options for styling hair involve heat—a great tool for making your client's hair look its best in the short-term, but the greatest culprit in causing all kinds of damage in years to come. Ninety-six percent of American homes have a blow dryer, and all salons do, but it's important to blow dry hair as little as possible to help retain moisture and keep from stressing hair or drying it out. The bottom line is that heat is your client's enemy. Try to avoid styling with heat. If you must style with heat, follow these tips: Use a heat-controlled blow dryer that evaporates moisture by diffusing the level of moisture. Stop drying hair before it's completely dry. After most of the style is set, let the rest dry on its own. Give hair a break and let it air dry. Also, look for styling products that have thermoguards that protect hair from heat the same way sunscreen protects skin from harmful rays.

You should train your clients to use the recommended products. Don't let them go home and read the instructions. Walk your clients through the process until they feel comfortable. It is important that you become a valuable educator on your client's team of the professionals she enlists for hair loss help, rather than just a salesperson.

Dry Ideas Stop Friction

In applying products, remember that wetter hair will dilute the product more, so the roots need to be dried first, then the ends, but don't dry it completely. When you blot or dry hair, leave it about three percent moist for optimal product absorption. There is a shammy product available now—aptly dubbed the friction-free towel—that blots hair and absorbs most of the moisture before you begin drying. Towel-drying hair can damage it—especially if it's thin or thinning. If you were to look at a towel under a microscope, you would see that it has looped threads. These threads grab and tear hair as the towel dries it. Even the fluffiest towel will hurt hair. In the absence of a shammy, your clients should be advised to blot their hair with paper towels after showering to avoid damage from a towel.

Something for Everyone

There are many styling tools designed to help women with thin and thinning hair. There is also a lot of misinformation regarding styling tools. Many people profess that thin hair can't take a lot of "product" or that products like conditioners will weigh down their hair. There is also talk about how you should shampoo hair but not over-cleanse it, or shampoo but not condition, so as not to give the hair an oily, dangling look. These concepts are not necessarily true. Do not be afraid to use products that will help your clients look their best. There are a lot of products that will help the health and the look of thin hair and those products should be used diligently in the styling process.

Read directions carefully (and advise your clients to, on their own) to ensure you use products properly and correctly. This is important, because many clients use these products incorrectly and are left with thin, droopy, lifeless hair—the complete opposite of what you are trying to achieve for them.

Products are grouped into a few different categories that build upon one another, so you should use them in order. Start with the right *cleansing and conditioning* products, which include quality shampoos and conditioners (thin, light, non-paraffin products that are used after every single shampoo). Work with a good-quality shampoo product devised for cleansing thin or thinning hair and developed to nurture the roots. Use conditioners that work specifically against hair splitting.

You will want to use the right products in *drying* hair. There are some that address roots, shafts, and ends separately, so you can isolate the areas your client is predominantly concerned with if you find that that works best. If you must blow dry hair or use tools that rely on heat, seek out blower and ironing products that use less heat and are less abrasive overall.

To set the style, you can use *finishing* products, such as pommades and sprays, for a truly polished look. Sprays should be light and non-drying to prevent breakage. There are sprays that also lift hair close to the root for more volume. For a lasting effect, apply light *lifting* products and encourage your clients to apply them throughout the day, the way they might reapply makeup to boost or freshen their look.

Advise your clients to talk to their dermatologists as well to make sure they have the well-rounded guidance that will allow them to work within the most appropriate product line for their personal needs.

CREAM AND POWDER

As light powders and liquids cover dark or red spots on skin, dark and light powders and liquids can cover thinning areas on scalps. If the right products are used, your clients can look nearly perfect and no one will notice their hair thinning and loss issues.

Your clients may be hesitant about these solutions. Late-night infomercials have consumers visualizing spraying color onto their scalps and hearing enthusiastic applause while they wonder if people are really serious or just mocking them. There's a big difference between effective camouflage makeup and spray-on color. The trick is to decipher all of the propaganda and truly understand how to approach the concealment of hair loss conditions.

The way to understand how to use camouflage makeup to hide hair loss and thinning is to first acknowledge that the skin on your clients' faces is very different from the skin that covers their scalps. The makeup for scalp coverage has to be designed so the skin on the scalp can absorb it. Scalp skin is harder to get through than facial skin.

> **MOST IDEAL FOR:**
>
> early Diffusion Grade I—10–20 percent thinning

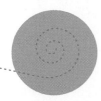

PRODUCT COMPARISONS

Here are some examples of camouflage options on the market today:

PRODUCT: Alopecia Masking Lotion

Application: Dab on with applicators, two minutes

Concept: Tinted cream is applied to thinning and open areas of scalp to create illusion of continual hair at the base of the scalp.

Cost: About $20 (variable length of supply)

Manufacturer: Spencer Forrest

PRODUCT: Topical Shading

Application: Pressed powder, dab on with applicator, two minutes or more

Concept: Tinted powder helps fill in where scalp is blank and swells hair shafts for fullness.

Cost: $30 for eight-month supply, but may need another color to blend properly

Manufacturer: DermMatch, Inc.

PRODUCT: Hair Building Fibers

Application: Shake on, 30 seconds

Concept: Tinted spray temporarily bonds appropriately tinted fibers to your thinning hair to create density throughout.

Cost: About $20–40 for 30–75 day supplies respectively

Manufacturer: Spencer Forrest

PRODUCT: Texturizing Spray Thickener

Application: Spray on, 30 seconds

Concept: Tinted spray covers bald spots and bonds fibers to your hair to create density and color throughout.

Cost: About $20

Manufacturer: Spencer Forrest

There are basically two scalp skin conditions: oily to normal and dry to normal. It is hard to get sprays on the scalp without getting them on hair too. If you use a spray makeup for the scalp, you will get flatter, darker hair and a cakey-looking scalp.

Beautiful Hair—How to Give It Back

Whether your client is on a date, at an important meeting, or on a rush-hour subway car, the effect can look pretty scary to people.

To prepare scalp skin for camouflage makeup, it's important to exfoliate the scalp once or twice a week. Here's where your partnership with your client comes into play. She will have to be informed of this at-home maintenance tip for the solution to work well. Otherwise, camouflaging can clog her pores and block hair growth. If you think exfoliating will create ruddiness, redness, and dandruff, or exacerbate flakiness caused by thyroid imbalances, think again. The last thing we would want is for your client to scratch her scalp. Aside from causing flakiness and dryness, it could further damage hair follicles at the root, or the roots themselves. Exfoliation should be done gently with the right product to easily lift off the makeup residue and clean pores properly. Training your client is key to striking the balance so that you are neither blocking growth with undue clogging nor preventing growth by undue scratching.

Cosmetic, camouflage-tints color in exposed scalp areas and some even create the illusion of additional hair fibers. They are said to hold up under perspiration and weather, and are washable. They look best on those who have lost a little or an intermediate amount of hair; those who have lost more hair are less likely to benefit from a natural appearance after application.

TIPS FOR SUCCESSFUL CAMOUFLAGING

When applying camouflage makeup, cover only the empty or emptier parts of the scalp. If your client has oily to normal skin on her scalp, the best product to use is a pressed powder. This eliminates shine and is absorbed well. If the skin on her scalp is dry to normal, try a cream that will help eliminate dryness. Both products do what we want them to: they go directly on the scalp and very little, if any, gets on the hair itself. They can also be blended to the shade of choice.

Lessons of the Great Televised Presidential Debate

Who can forget the 1960 Presidential debate in which runny studio makeup on Nixon's white shirt really made an unfavorable impression on the people watching? One concern about using camouflage makeup is that when it rains or when your client sweats, there's a good chance the product will come off. The last thing your client wants is to be out in public and have color running down her face onto her clothes. Test a small amount of the product you are considering on the back of her hand and, after it dries or sets, see if you can wipe it off with a moist towel or tissue. The product that is least likely to wipe off is the best one for her. The trick is to choose a camouflage makeup product that suits her lifestyle. If she is extremely active, her makeup should contain a certain level of pigment stain to prevent it from running.

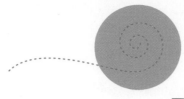

EYELASHES AND EYEBROWS WITHOUT BATTING A SINGLE EYELASH

Eyebrows and eyelashes thin and fall out too. This is hair loss, after all, and many women are devastated by it. Advise your client not to go to sleep with her eye makeup still on, because in the morning, some of her eyelashes will have either fallen out or broken off. Ultimately, as with so many poor choices we make in how we take care of ourselves, if this choice becomes a regular habit, the total effect will only be obvious to her later when it is harder to correct.

Further, if your client tweezes too zealously and her eyebrows aren't growing back, she might consider some of the options that are more readily available today than they were in the pencil-happy "Hollywood Glam" era of the early part of the last century. There are semi-permanent powders or pencils to simulate eyelashes or eyebrows—which means that they won't wash away quickly, but can be taken off regularly. Stencils come in different cuts and shapes, which allow you to draw eyebrows with a practiced slight-imprecision for the most natural effect that can stay on for a week at a time. There is also henna for eyelashes and eyebrows, which is the most natural "tattooing" possible, offering natural pigmentation that can sometimes be combined with stenciling. Or you can offer permanent makeup, which is the most expensive and the most demanding for an experienced, artistic professional to apply. Study and practice carefully if you are interested in making this one of your specialties. In certain cases, henna and permanent makeup products are used to even out hairlines, although these methods are less successful on the scalp than on the face.

Remind your client not to go for the permanent makeup before gradually building on the more temporary methods to find the right shades and styles, and to become more comfortable with the new shape, texture, and color of her restored eyebrows. Thinking things through carefully will equip your client with the wherewithal to choose the right options. Don't let her make rash decisions about doing something permanent to her face. Be the voice of reason if she is looking for a quick fix that can't be undone. Which brings us to . . .

YOUR PROFESSIONAL RESPONSIBILITY

The camouflage makeup artist who works best with thinning hair or completely blank areas is one with theater training, or a cosmetic therapist trained specifically to deal with these issues. If you have burn or scar coverage experience, then you would also be a good choice for a woman to consult for camouflaging. Be prepared to offer references or your credentials if clients wish to consult them.

If you have worked at a makeup-counter, that doesn't automatically make you the ideal candidate to effectively camouflage women who experience hair loss, and if you are a salon makeup artist, you may not be practiced in these methods. Don't take them on without working on your skills and educating yourself regarding products on the market and how they should be applied. If you are not interested in specializing in this solution, your clients may still turn to you in the hope that you may be a good source to help them find the specialist who will be able to work with them. Learn what you can about the professionals in your geographic area with respectable reputations in camouflage so that you can offer suggestions that will make your clients happy. Taking time to connect with these other professionals so that you can develop mutual business will be beneficial for both of you. This personal connection will also help your mutual clients, because you will both strive to maintain a good working relationship with each other by making sure any clients that have been referred to you are happy—an additional reason to be a thorough and accommodating professional in dealing with clients.

If you are an esthetician, or work with one who can help combat the challenges of facial hair thinning and loss, that puts you in a particularly specialized professional category. The best estheticians to deal with more comprehensive hair loss and thinning issues are either going to be very specialized with experience in the subject, or be certified in hair replacement programs. They may be more helpful with cleansing, conditioning, and massage than with camouflage makeup in some cases.

Cream Camouflage Step-By-Step Procedure

CREAM CAMOUFLAGE TOOL LIST

cream camouflage   sponge   comb

Comb the hair away from the area(s) to be masked. The hair may be either damp or dry, but application is easier on a damp scalp.

Put a small amount of cream camouflage on the edge of the applicator sponge. Using the applicator sponge, gently rub cream camouflage lightly onto the scalp where the hair is thinning. Be sure to blend into the surrounding hair for a totally natural appearance. Comb the hair back over the area and instantly you will see a thicker head of hair. You may immediately proceed to comb, brush, or blow dry.

Once completely dry (about five minutes), cream camouflage will not readily come off with water or perspiration. You can even wear it swimming. Cream camouflage removes easily with any shampoo.

It is important to apply cream camouflage directly to the scalp, without getting too much on the hair. Cream camouflage bonds more durably to the scalp than to hair. A little cream camouflage on the base of the hair will thicken it and look great, but if you get too much on the hair, you may experience some rub-off.

Applying cream camouflage to a thinning frontal area takes more care. When masking the front, start farther back and move forward, making sure that there is very little cream camouflage left on the applicator when you reach the frontal hairline area. For extremely thin areas, use a small amount of cream camouflage and spread it thinly over the area. You may blot off the excess with a tissue, and pat the remainder onto the scalp. The thinning appearance will be noticeably reduced.

Beautiful Hair—How to Give It Back

Have clients use cream camouflage every day if possible. The more they use cream camouflage the more adept they will get at its application, and the more natural their results. If necessary, have them practice different techniques to see which works best.

Profile: . . . . Laura

Age: 39

Laura had always had thin hair, but in the last few years, after childbirth, and while working in the hairdressing business, she noticed the elevated stress level produced by her lifestyle. An increase in the amount of hair she saw in the sink on a daily basis concerned her deeply. While Laura knew she didn't need a hair replacement, she tried what she could to get her hair to look fuller and act more responsive to restoration treatments. Yet she still didn't have that bounce and fullness that even her thin hair would normally give her. She started to be able to see more of her scalp. She was especially concerned because she worked under the lights and intensity of a salon, and there was the added pressure of having to have hair that looked good since clients would notice her hair if it didn't look good.

In her case, it was decided that a pressed powder camouflage for her oilier skin was a good coverage option, and it also gave a lift to the root area that added fullness when she styled her hair. She feels like herself again, and no longer feels self-conscious at the salon's busy front desk.

Pressed Powder Camouflage Step-by-Step Procedure

PRESSED POWDER CAMOUFLAGE TOOL LIST

pressed powder camouflage	sponge	water spritz bottle	comb

Start with a clean, dry scalp. If the hair is damp, that is OK. It is best to apply pressed powder camouflage before getting dressed. A brightly lit bathroom sink and mirror are good for application. Wet your applicator.

Rub your damp applicator in the container. Rub in circular motions. Make sure the colored powder is accumulating on the applicator tip. A brand new disc may need a little extra water and rubbing.

Rub your applicator directly on the scalp. Color one small area at a time. If you are applying along the front hairline, color behind the hairline, never in front of it. Create a soft, natural hairline by fading the edge of your client's color. Use a dry applicator and rub gently along the edge of the color so that color fades gradually toward the forehead. Continue applying until all exposed areas are colored evenly. Keep your applicator damp as you rub again in the container for more colored powder.

When you are done coloring the area, brush or comb your client's hair right away while it's still damp from application. This distributes the pressed powder in the area of application so it can coat and thicken any thin hairs. Now your application needs to dry. If you normally blow dry, use low heat and low wind. Otherwise, brushing or combing every few minutes will speed drying. The hair roots are the last to dry, so be sure to brush or comb down to the roots. This helps maximize the hair's fullness. The application is dry when it's dry to the roots.

When your application is completely dry, brush the hair thoroughly. Use a firm, salon-quality brush. Brush down to the roots and out to the ends. Thorough brushing of a dried application gives a final lift to thin hairs now coated and thickened by pressed powder camouflage. It also helps remove any excess pressed powder camouflage from the hair.

If any excess powder gets on the client's forehead, wipe it with a tissue. Wet wipes or rubbing alcohol on a paper towel work well for the back of the neck and shoulders. If there is excess powder on the clothing, don't touch it. Shake it off or blast it off with a blow dryer. Use any shampoo to remove pressed powder camouflage.

Beautiful Hair—How to Give It Back

Topical, Pharmaceutical, and Nutritional Solutions

INTRODUCTION

We live in a world in which consumers are increasingly made aware of what they're buying. Women with hair loss are faced with an array of bottles of stuff on the market. The questions they are asking are valid: What can you trust? What really works? What are the consequences of following the directions when it comes to all the possible products and treatments that promise renewed hair growth and preservation? What will be a waste of time, effort, and finances? What is worth trying when the result can't be guaranteed? Granted, when dealing with the possibility of losing more hair, this is one journey women are often willing to make, whether they find themselves at the beginning of noticing some thinning or further down the hair loss road. Yet, this huge unknown can seem a tough gamble when there is so much at stake.

But two things are certain: one is that trying some of these options makes sense before moving forward with more comprehensive measures (or even while your clients are grappling with other more complex solutions); the other is that whatever we—and our clients—do try, we need to follow the directions and use these methods correctly. If we don't, the result can be problematic. It is your responsibility as the professional to be up to speed on what the latest

> **MOST IDEAL FOR:**
> ....
> all Diffusion Grades;
> Highly Recommended:
> Diffusion Grades I & II—
> 10–50 percent
> thinning or loss.

products are on the market and how they should and shouldn't be used. It is your client's responsibility to listen carefully to your instructions and follow them at home, and do her own research so that the responsibility for her well-being does not rest entirely on your shoulders.

If there were an absolute cure for hair loss, this book would not need to be written, and your clients would be standing in line for the miracle solution at this very moment. So while that one proven product may be in someone's laboratory somewhere, there are proven methods we do know about, and there are also those we believe can work well, even though scientific study may not yet have proclaimed those methods foolproof.

As discussed in previous chapters, research has taught us that hair loss is not due to one single cause, but we do know specific things we can do about it. If you want to begin to treat hair loss, begin with these solutions, and continue them during later stages of loss to stimulate growth and maintain growing hair. But it will take maintenance and persistence. This vigilance is parallel to that which is required in treating an ailment like diabetes: there are initial levels of treatment followed by more progressive levels. If your clients don't empower themselves and take care of themselves on a long-term basis, the treatments they've tried will not have the effect they were going for to begin with, and what you and they have already done may prove to have been a waste of everyone's time. Your client has to commit

Beautiful Hair—How to Give It Back

herself to continued care in order for these potential solutions to bring about lasting results. That being said, don't let your client stay up late for the television infomercials, memorizing toll-free numbers as they reach for the phone. A lot of products on the market have a placebo effect. What it comes down to is the basics of nutrition, physical care, treatment, and therapy. And let's not forget about patience. Nothing happens overnight in hair loss treatment.

Certain topical treatments, pharmaceutical programs, and nutritional possibilities can help to maintain a healthy scalp, keep existing, growing hair, and potentially restore hair that has already been lost. Options involving nutrition and treatments like massage therapy are geared toward affecting the problem at a sub-dermal level, whereas topical treatment works from the outside in.

Profile: .... Robin

Occupation: Radio and television personality

As a result of her hand-held laser treatments and her use of other topical products to restore her hair, Robin experienced terrific results, as evidenced in her letter to her specialists. She wrote: "How can I ever thank you enough for helping me love my hair again? I have tried myriad products, but never experienced the results achieved with a hair treatment regime. From the very first intense treatment you performed at your salon, the results were visible. I continue to see the results daily as I use the products at home. I used to be a slave to the whims of my hair—but thanks to you and the proper selected treatment for my hair—I am in charge!!!

Profile: .... Gail

Occupation: Housewife

Gail had just finished a six-month chemotherapy treatment series that had resulted in the loss of all her hair. During that period of no hair, she looked as natural as if she had her own hair because she had been fitted with a human-hair wig. But now, she wanted her hair back as soon as possible in the best condition.

Through an intensified treatment program of laser light therapy combined with hair vitamins, scalp message therapy, and revitalizing topical scalp treatment, her hair re-growth was stimulated to its optimum level growth potential.

"When my hair started to grow back so slowly after the chemotherapy it seemed like it would take a lifetime to regain my full head of hair. I heard of so many products and vitamins that everyone said would work, or that were advertised to grow hair, it made me so confused. Through the knowledge I received in my consultation with you and then the results that made me see the light at the end of the tunnel, I would go to my support group meetings and I was out of my wig and wearing my own hair. Months before the others would even consider unveiling their new growth. This not only took away the long endured pain of waiting as I continued to look into the mirror for the head of hair I once had, but it gave me hope each and every day. Thank you and your staff for helping me look myself again."

NUTRITION

With iron deficiency, hormonal imbalances, and thyroid ailments being heavy contributors to the causes regarding hair thinning and hair loss, it's easy to see how nutritional factors can play an important role in addressing the problem. Specialists should always have in mind

Beautiful Hair—How to Give It Back

that the body is an incredible machine. It takes in foods and nutrients and uses them to care for all the body's needs. After it applies the various elements that have been consumed to the needs of all the different parts, it makes its way to the last recipients: hair and nails. When your client takes supplements, she gets the benefits at more intense levels at the outset, as they travel throughout the body. They are muted toward the end, when they finally reach the hair. As a result, scientists have designed supplements to carry low levels of vitamins that make hair grow; they contain amino acids that help to hold the effective intensity until the end of their course.

The result, however, is that it may take as long as 90 days for hair to respond, so it will be a long-term endeavor on your client's part. Of course, long-term is a relative measure—consider the potential life and outcome of hair loss concerns and 90 days may seem a drop in the proverbial bucket of time. But the results you and your client want to achieve in using nutritional means to combat the problem of hair loss is to slow down the loss, increase growth, and, finally, strengthen that growth so that it can be relied upon and is long-lasting. In short, it takes time to gain time.

According to a recent study conducted by the International Food Information Council, a whopping 93 percent of Americans believe certain foods offer health benefits that go above and beyond simple nutrition and may actually reduce the risk of various health concerns. Yet, it's hard to find people who are eating what they are supposed to for the best possible nutritional outcome. And today, women are pressed for time and find themselves balancing a number of roles and responsibilities. There's a lot of eating on the run, eating less to compensate for poor habits, eating fast, consuming a lot of chemically processed foods, and other factors.

Eating right is one of the best ways to repair hair. But with things the way they are today, supplements have become increasingly important. However, you should be wary in recommending supplements. Advise your client against buying products from generic companies that may have developed supplements for hair as just another element in a line they claim is a complete health system.

Drinking supplemental drinks can be helpful since they are already in liquid form and will travel faster through the body. Taking liquid vitamins also works well for the same reason. They are more likely to be absorbed than non-liquid vitamins because they don't have to be broken down first and manipulated, so they are less likely to be lost in the process of digestion or eliminated before they can be used. The idea, according to Dr. Gary Ross, who has written on the subject for *Healthy Hair* magazine, is to capture essential amino acids in the form of supplements, which the body can't manufacture but which the hair follicles need in order to continually produce keratin—the protein that makes up hair.

Dr. Ross also explains the benefits of biotin in helping to prevent thinning and loss by keeping the hair and scalp from becoming too dry. B-complex vitamins, such as pantothenic acid, which are often found in (but too often also lost in the cooking of) foods like organ meats, egg yolks, and cheese, also keep hair from graying and aging. Saw palmetto is cited as a substance that helps stop DHT production.

Viviscal is one example of a supplement that has been reported to show increased hair growth and strength. The tablets contain refined marine protein, vitamin C, and silica derived from plants, and are geared toward easing the blockage of nutrient flow to the scalp. Viviscal is aggressively marketed to complement laser light therapy.

Beautiful Hair—How to Give It Back

Yet, the bottom line, as with so many health issues, is for your client to be careful with her diet. When addressing this issue, it is important that you do so sensitively, mentioning it as a suggestion in a way that can't be negatively personalized. Keeping the health benefit of eating right at the forefront of the discussion is preferred to discussing any kind of weight control measure or allowing the conversation to be misconstrued to mean that you may be hinting at weight loss. You are not. One of the primary reasons for keeping the discussion health-oriented is that eating disorders may arise among women who are overly self-conscious about their weight. Some of your clients may already have eating disorders that could be made worse by your "eating-right" discussion. Keep it simple, scientific, and hair-loss-oriented when discussing proper nutrition. Eating disorders may contribute to hair loss, so correcting those issues—and other issues, such as hypo- or hyper-thyroidism, which is diet-related—is a first step in tackling the hair loss problem and safeguarding your client's general health. The importance of a balanced diet can't be overstated, utilizing foods rich in omega 3 fatty acids (such as salmon) and proteins, sulfur (dairy, eggs, fish), zinc, and B-complex, A, C, and F vitamins. If your client does eat a balanced, healthy diet, she will often set a strong foundation to receive the nutrients she needs to at least begin to keep her hair healthy. Then she can supplement from there. Eating well could also eliminate stress, which can contribute to hair thinning and loss. And, of course, proper exercise along with better nutrition will only help things, by increasing circulation and improving overall health.

SUPPLEMENTS AND VITAMINS

Many people are told the myth that you need to load your system up with one vitamin or another for the health of your hair. This is simply not true. It's important for your clients to take a multi-faceted approach to improving nutrition in the interest of hair health. The ultimate achievement would be to strike a true balance between medical and holistic approaches in order to round out the picture and treat hair loss from both of these important angles.

A good rule of thumb in terms of food intake is that whatever is good for the heart is going to be good for the hair. That means eating a low-fat diet that is not extreme in carbohydrate or protein consumption. If your client is enjoying a healthy heart diet, she is already employing a healthy hair diet. We know that the blood supply to the heart is essential for its survival. The heart of the hair follicle is the papilla, which supplies the blood that creates keratin for the hair. So the papilla is the major vessel supplying this essential material to the hair follicle. Keeping that flow healthy and intact is very important, and the papilla responds similarly to the way blood vessels do in achieving that aim.

There are a host of supplement manufacturers, but the products of three major players have been found to be the best in producing positive effects while treating hair loss issues. There's Phytologie—a French company that manufactures plant-based products containing the amino acids we discussed—namely Phytophanere, a supplement to be taken for four months that addresses lifeless hair and is a companion product to thinning hair treatments. There is also Viviscal, which balances the body, scalp, and blood flow in its approach, and Hair Support, which produces a product called hair vitamins to use in conjunction with other topical treatments in its line.

Another company, Nisim International, offers a comprehensive hair stimulating extract, which contains herbs, amino acids, and biotin, among other helpful supplements. General Nutrition Centers and other more generic manufacturers also offer hair supplement systems, but the first three described above are the most active companies on the supplement market.

THE AT-HOME TREATMENT PROGRAM

Treating hair loss actually starts at home, where it can have a profound effect on the way your client lives. The products your client will use at home will change. The way she takes care of her hair, and even the way she does many standard things in her life, will change to accommodate the needs of her hair. More specifically, at home, on her own, is where she will most likely begin to chart her course of treatment and monitor her needs in order to have the most effective outcome.

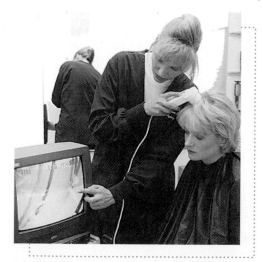

About a week before your clients come to see you, have them gather and count the hair that falls out. When they come in, you can conduct an analysis, using a microscopic video monitoring of their scalp, the follicles, the opening where the hair emerges from the scalp, and other factors, and then you can do an assessment of the products your clients will need.

Your client needs to count the hair she's lost in order to measure and put a value on the stage of her loss so that she can, in turn, understand what steps she needs to take to alter the situation. If she collects hair she has lost and puts it in a clear plastic baggie, daily, for a week, she can see at a glance whether she is losing more or less hair as time goes on. She can then show you the hair collected and share the results with you so you can move forward together.

Evaluate various factors at different times to see how the problems are progressing. You should note that hair loss is related to what happened yesterday—not today. Your client will likely have forgotten what might have caused it, because the loss only becomes noticeable *after* the events that triggered it. Encourage your clients to keep a diary or a journal of their hair loss over a ninety-day period, which represents the cycle of hair. Suggest that they begin journaling before they begin addressing their hair loss concerns constructively, and continue after.

For the same reasons, you should take two-to-five-year personal histories on clients in your initial consultation and create a timeline showing the correlation of events in their lives with noticed amounts of loss. When your clients see these timelines, they will say, "I didn't realize that all of this was happening at the same time." The main reason to do that initial assessment is to win the first half of the battle—understanding what has actually happened that brought about some of these issues.

You can take clients through a training program with products you recommend after the initial consultation. Show them how to use products, and give them targeted instructions. They will leave feeling responsible for monitoring what happens. They should log their activities as they can, including major events and occurrences, medications they take, foods they eat, and more.

Recommend that they incorporate massage into their program twice daily—once in the morning and once at night, especially during a stressful day. Tell them to drink a lot of water, which helps their circulation and eliminates blockages. Encourage them to routinely brush their hair for good hair-care maintenance.

SALON TREATMENTS: Experts Work Their Magic

Although your clients can learn how to use special products to exfoliate hair follicles at home, visiting a salon or center where an esthetician or specialist does it for them allows for more advanced exfoliating through the application of technological methods. The specialist will perform a deep follicular cleansing—a little more complex than a scalp "facial"—and comprehensive conditioning, and will apply an astringent-like scalp stimulant. Then he or she will treat the scalp with an ointment that your client can also use on her own during the day for a moisturizing effect. It's important to advise your client not to overuse the moisturizing ointment, so proper training for self-application is key. Investigating this specialty or hiring someone with this specialty may boost your business and provide an often-missing element of treatment among salons and centers. Finally, certain salons may use laser light therapy, which is the most advanced form of salon treatment. This treatment is worth examining and potentially incorporating into your treatment services.

LASER LIGHT THERAPY

Unlike some of the other solutions covered in this chapter, low-level laser light therapy—or photo therapy, as some call it—may be more appropriate for women who have experienced *recent* hair loss. The treatment itself is essentially a set amount of time spent under laser light targeted to stimulate blood flow in the scalp and strengthen the hair follicle and hair shaft.

One company, Harmonix Corporation, distributes a laser light therapy program involving 20 actual treatments over the course of a year, specialized vitamins, a follow-up shampoo and conditioner combo, a topical enzymatic solution, and some-times the use of a specialized shower filter to dechlorinate water that reaches your hair in the shower. The entire program costs nearly $3,000 for a year. Other laser therapy programs may cost significantly less, depending upon what the program includes, your clients' individual needs, and who is administer-ing the therapy.

Oyvind Berg, founder and president of Harmonix, Corp., says laser light therapy works particularly well at stopping the progression of hair loss among women, especially those experi-encing hormonal imbalances, such as menopause. But it's not a miracle cure.

"Hair loss doesn't happen overnight, so you can't rectify it overnight," says Berg. "Most of our clients sign up for six months to a year, and we ask them to be prepared to spend a year with us for therapies administered twice a week for the first six to eight weeks, once for the next six to eight weeks, and then for a reevaluation after we've seen the results and are able to recom-mend a practical maintenance program or additional therapy, if necessary." According to Berg, the cost of the therapy ranges

from $3,000–4,000, and includes products that are recommended for maintenance during the process.

"We've developed a line of products we recommend because they are free of chemicals that may further harm hair already at risk," says Berg. "And there are other products we recommend, like Rogaine. We want to apply what we can to solve the problem over the course of the treatment period for the best possible result." Harmonix also trains professionals to administer their laser light therapy, and that training can be done during a three-to-four day seminar or, for more advanced specialists, over a longer time period for more intense education and practice. Harmonix advises women who are interested to ask the staff of any center how long they have been providing the laser light therapy, if they have a doctor on staff or an affiliation with a doctor (which is not necessary, but which helps to define the credibility of the program they offer), and if they have information readily available regarding the efficacy and safety of the program.

The Harmonix laser is a 30-dial rotational device that looks a bit like a hairdryer. You sit under it for 15 to 30 minutes, feeling no particular sensation, while the light stimulation causes microcirculation to improve, bringing nutrients back to hair follicles so the hair can grow again. According to Berg, improvement varies from moderate to full regrowth, depending upon the individual.

Another company, Laser Hair Care, claims to help reduce hair loss within six to nine treatments. The company cites scientific research that showed an overwhelmingly positive response in a group of men treated by laser therapy to stop hair loss. The client is treated while seated under a helmet apparatus (similar to an old-fashioned hair dryer) that has a rotating cap emitting laser light. Side effects may include a prickly sensation during treatment and an ensuing greasy scalp condition, according to the company.

One of the important things to understand is that laser light therapy is indeed a program—if your client opts for laser treatment, she should use follow-up products and continue the treatment over the course of the prescribed time period. It's not a one-shot deal and it requires maintenance.

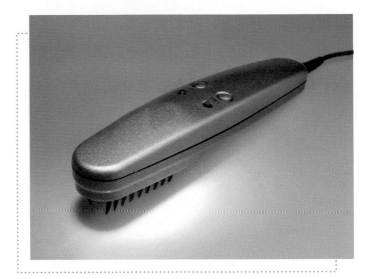

HairMax also markets a revolutionary product that has had proven results and that works easily at home. The laser comb is basically a handheld, cold-laser-producing "brush" that you use or your client uses for a few minutes at a time a couple of times a week. Over a period of weeks, she may notice that hair loss is slowed significantly. Some have reported noticing regrowth after use of the laser comb as well. Operating on the theory that hair grows faster during summer's long daylight hours, the comb delivers stimulating light to hair follicles in the scalp and re-energizes them. The comb costs a few hundred dollars, but may save money in treatments over the long run. You can offer this service in your salon or sell the laser comb with proper instruction to your client and follow-up sessions with you.

Consider the future of laser light therapy. With pending FDA approval as a medical treatment, Berg says he believes lasers will become increasingly available. "There will be a proliferation of lasers to where they become utility pieces of equipment in most salons and spas," says Berg. "Then people will be able to use lasers to stop hair loss at a much earlier stage."

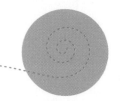

TOPICAL PHARMACEUTICAL TREATMENT

A few major brands of topical pharmaceutical treatments are being marketed to women today, the most prominent of which is *Rogaine*. Although I am not endorsing *Rogaine*, it has been found to be successful in regrowing hair. However, if treatment is discontinued, regrown hair will be lost within a few months at most. It is not true, however, that a woman will lose more hair after stopping treatment, at least not as a result of ceasing use of the product. A woman should only use *Rogaine* if she knows she is experiencing hereditary hair loss, or **Androgenetic Alopecia**.

According to the Women's Institute for Fine and Thinning Hair, *Rogaine* for Women, when tested clinically, was reported to show regrowth after eight months in two out of three women. The product is applied to the scalp after washing and drying hair and it works by keeping hair growing for a longer period of time than it would in its normal cycle of growth. The company recommends using *Rogaine* twice a day; results reportedly begin showing between four and eight months. Minor side effects are listed as scalp irritation and itching. Another drawback users have reported, although it is disputed by some professionals, is that it is possible that if *Rogaine* gets below the hairline onto the forehead or face, the user may grow hair there as well. To be safe, careful application is strongly recommended. That means your client also has to be careful that her scalp is fairly dry before applying it, so that none of the solution runs off onto her face and neck. *Rogaine* is applied with an applicator that is part of the packaging and it is rubbed into the scalp. Then the person applying it washes her hands very well afterwards. The makers of Rogaine caution pregnant and nursing women to avoid using the product since women in those circumstances were not included in testing. It's available over the counter for about $25 a month.

According to Dr. Wilma Bergfeld, head of Clinical Research in Dermatology at the Cleveland Clinic Foundation in Cleveland, Ohio, a stronger (five percent) concentration of *Rogaine* works better for women than the more diluted version, but it can increase facial hair in some. Reducing dosage or discontinuing use solves the problem. Also, according to Dr. Bergfeld, scaly or itchy scalp is the largest problem seen associated with the use of the product, but it can be treated with an over-the-counter hydrocortisone cream or a prescription hydrocortisone solution.

"*Rogaine* grows hair between 50 and 60 percent of the time. If used in compliance, it can be a good agent [for regrowth]. But regrowth activity plateaus at one year," says Dr. Bergfeld.

And if the product's use is discontinued, hair will go back to its baseline rate of loss. So when you hear people talking about how discontinuing use of *Rogaine* may cause hair to fall out even more, that may appear so because hair may be naturally shedding at a faster rate or be further along on the scale of loss than it was when the person was first starting to use the product.

Propecia (also known as *Finasteride*) is another option, in the form of pills to be swallowed. However, women who are interested in becoming pregnant cannot use it because it has

How to Count the Hair Dismount

For the least speculative approach to estimating amounts of hair lost, advise your client to do the following for her assessment: Take clear plastic baggies and, with permanent marker, note the date for the week on the front of each. Take hair that comes off in the shower, on your pillow, on your brush, off your shoulders, and off your clothes, and place it throughout the week in that week's marked baggie. Don't go crazy with exact counts, just take a general, relaxed count at week's end and mark the number on the baggie. You don't have to do a hair-by-hair physical count, but, rather, a more visual count—in other words, try to basically size up the situation. Note also that as you incorporate massage into your at-home treatment, you may see an increase in the amount of hair you are losing, but don't freak out—it's only a temporary response to new movement and stimulation. Products that catch the hair as you shower, called drain catchers, are available to help in this effort (you, as the specialist, can sell these in your salon).

been found to cause birth defects in male offspring, namely having to do with the health of male hormones and genitalia. Future moms must stay away. According to the folks at Medical Hair Restoration, women interested in giving birth should not even touch a broken tablet.

Minoxidil is an oral medication that needs to be taken twice daily. Clinical studies conducted by Pharmacia and Upjohn reported that it appeared to work best on those who are younger and are experiencing the earlier stages of hair loss. Of those tested, almost 20 percent of the women that were between the ages of 18 and 45 saw moderate regrowth, while another 40 percent showed minimal regrowth. One drawback is that some professionals are reluctant to back the success of the product, claiming it usually helps grow only short, fine hair, rather than hair like you would normally have on your head. The same side effects as those seen with *Rogaine* for Women are seen with *Minoxidil:* potentially itchy scalp and automatic reversal of regrowth upon discontinuation of use.

NuGen HP is another company that produces solutions that are marketed in competition with *Rogaine* and *Propecia*. Theirs is a two-step system that incorporates a follicle enhancer to be used twice daily and massaged in, and what is called a turbo accelerator, which is a topical vitamin product to be absorbed into the inside of your client's wrist, once a day, also through massage. There is the same itching side effect issue as described in the other treatments above, and use must be continued over time, although not as frequently after hair is restored. It is also formulated to combat dihydrotestosterone (DHT), a hormone formed when the enzyme 5alpha-reductose interacts with testosterone.

Spencer Forrest offers a product called the Folligen Solution Therapy Spray, which it markets as a tool for women experiencing low estrogen and menopause-related hair loss. It was developed by Dr. Loren Pickart, who also developed another successful hair-growth inducer, *Tricomin*.

Cortisone injection can also trigger hair regrowth, and is used primarily for those afflicted with **Alopecia Areata**, according to Dr. Bergfeld. The injection puts the cortisone in the area of the growing hair follicle at the anogen bulb base, which then reduces inflammation and, in many people, allows hair to grow. The treatment has been used with some success by people with inflammatory scalp diseases, such as lupus arythematosus and lichen plano pilaris. Another group of inflammatory diseases it can be used for are those which fall under folliculitis decalvis.

Cortisone injections are administered every four to six weeks in series of three by dermatologists or specially trained nurses, according to Dr. Bergfeld. At the end of that time, the treatment success and need for continuance are assessed. The injections can be administered until hair is regrown, although they are moderately expensive. They are rarely given for common hereditary **Alopecia**. Says Dr. Bergfeld, "When all else fails, they can be used; but they are not considered the first mode of therapy."

YOUR RESPONSIBILITY

If your client is interested in this potential solution, she should certainly consult her doctor. You should be aware of the treatment, as well as the other pharmaceutical treatments, but remember that you are not a medical specialist. Be prepared to suggest one or two doctors in your vicinity that have good reputations in this area. Consult national dermatological and medical association Web sites to begin your search, and then ask the doctors if they have clients who will vouch for their success so you can recommend the doctors to your clients. Use your good sense in determining who is reliable, as the results of your recommendation will involve the health of your client and the future of your own reputation.

NATURAL TOPICAL TREATMENTS

Essential oils have also been reported to be helpful in treating hair loss. People have been known to mix oils such as

Scalp Massage—Getting the Juices Flowing

Self-administering a scalp massage is one of the best things your client can do for her hair. Increasing blood circulation to the tissue supporting the hair follicles will go a long way in keeping them healthy and productive. Nutrients from the blood will keep hair healthy.

To do this right, your client should avoid aggressive rubbing that will cause potentially harmful friction to her scalp. She will want to give herself a gentle but stimulating massage. Instruct her to do the following: Use your fingertips and rub with light to moderate pressure in a circular motion, covering the entire head one section at a time, from hairline and above ears, over the crown, and down to the nape of your neck. If you try to keep your head lower than the level of your heart, or hang your head slightly downward, that will allow gravity to assist in bringing blood circulation to your head in a shorter time. If you do this even once a day, it will be beneficial. But if you can give yourself a scalp massage two or three times a day, that will be even more beneficial.

jojoba, rosemary, lavender, and others, and apply the mixture to their scalps overnight. One woman who experienced hair loss, Melanie Von Zabuesnig, claims her concoction of certain amounts of the above oils mixed together restored her hair within six months, despite her long-term battle with **Alopecia** and her resulting near-baldness. Sesame oil, garlic, and ginger have also been reported as potential stimulants to help restore hair. Research isn't conclusive on this subject, but if you are interested in offering homeopathic remedies to your clients, you should consult a homeopathic specialist for further direction.

With so many potential options, which way is the current moving with hair thinning and loss? "Many women are moving

Beautiful Hair—How to Give It Back

toward some of the cosmetic products sold in salons, like *Nioxin*, and there are some advertisements on the Web for saw palmetto skin lotions and shampoos as well as biotin products," says Dr. Bergfeld. "Women are looking at biotin because we use it orally at this time. Nutritional supplements appear to be helpful both as antiinflammatories that enhance growth and as anti-anagens. While there are no real studies—just animal studies and some others—I have seen success in some individual female patients with anagen excess."

INTRODUCTION TO HAIR REPLACEMENT

So far we've discussed hair restoration solutions—the options that will help you to help your client maintain the hair she still has and potentially restore some of the hair she has lost. But sometimes restoration measures are not enough. The styling worked okay, but didn't cut it. The camouflaging wasn't the total answer. The topical treatments and therapies and the change in your client's diet will take time to take effect, and right now you both need other ideas—fast. Or perhaps the Diffusion Grade and pattern stage that you have identified render the previous solutions too mild for your client's circumstances.

If any of the above are true, these next few solutions for hair replacement will be quite helpful to you and your client. You will begin to understand the other possibilities that will help your client turn her life around, and you will read about women who have incorporated those solutions into their lives and experienced their own personal metamorphoses. Understanding these choices, which can be uniquely customized to your client's needs and desires, is a step toward getting back on that path to who she really is.

From here forward, you will learn about how you can use replacement hair to make your client's hair longer and fuller, or to cover thinning areas of her scalp. You will examine options for covering areas of loss with new hair or fashionable accessories, rather than with camouflage makeup. You will begin to understand all the ways that you can help a woman integrate new hair with her own, so that she is not covering her own beautiful hair, and what kinds of options she will see on the market if she chooses to wear a wig, a modern prosthetic, or a sleek hair addition or accessory. You will be educated about the kinds of surgeries and what your client will need to know before she talks to her doctors and surgeons, in order to have a safe transplant or other procedure. In short, you will learn how to help your client move forward to the next level of options, find what best suits her needs, and have a smarter sense of what other specialists may be available to your client.

There have been many advances in hair replacement over the years, and you are the lucky one who gets to bear the good news regarding how your client can reap the benefits of new products and technology. Women who were in her shoes 20 years ago might have literally flipped their wigs for these new-fangled possibilities.

SOLUTION 4

EXTENSIONS— Adding Hair in All Directions

AN EXTENSION OF HOLLYWOOD

It's not as though extensions are a new concept—people have been wearing them for years. But more recently, celebrities have incorporated them into their styling strategies—sometimes doing so subtly. As evidenced by some popular diva looks, extensions are the newest smoldering-hot fashion accessory.

This is exciting for women with thinning hair. With their celebrity status, extensions have thrashed their way into the mainstream market, becoming more accessible, acceptable, coveted, and admired. Yet, even with that explosion, women concerned with their loss of hair need to be aware of the pluses and minuses that go along with using extensions.

The biggest "pro" of new extension popularity is that there may be more choices of extensions to select from. The biggest "con" may be that a lot of mainstream stylists are beginning to apply them. Mainstream applications are not geared for women with thinning and weakening hair.

Extensions are a great option for your client if the condition of her existing hair is fair to good; she has lost no more than 20 percent of her hair (meaning you have

MOST IDEAL FOR:

Diffusion Grade I— 10–20 percent hair thinning or loss. Also ideal for those who simply desire more length and volume given her a Diffusion Grade of I after assessing her earlier); she wants to replace the look of what she lost; she does not suffer from weak hair due to medical illness or medical treatment; and she wants to add length, fullness, color, or texture to her growing hair. If she is hesitant about using what we call a hair system— many extensions attached to an undetectable fabric that allows her own hair to come through and be seen—extensions may be the winning answer. They can be daily wear (clip-on) or extended wear (secured through safe attachment systems described in this chapter). Still, she has reason to be careful. Extensions can sometimes be damaging, both in terms of the procedure used to apply them and the extension products themselves.

BAD BRAIDS AND WICKED WEAVES

Medical journals have reported that braiding and weaving extensions into hair can cause **traction alopecia** after hair follicles die from the pressure exerted upon them in the application process and afterward. African-American women have experienced this problem after using extensions for elaborate, artistic hairstyles for long time periods. Dr. Mirmirani, the foremost authority on hair loss among African-American women, attested to that fact. She cautions women to have appropriate extensions properly applied and maintained. Clips used for applying extensions can also cause **track alopecia** if they are constantly used or applied with a lot of tension in the same area over and over again.

Bosley Medical, a hair restoration treatment center with 28 years of experience, refers on its Web site to the "heavy price" people pay for using extensions. "The problem is that you can experience additional permanent hair loss from the frequent retying or tightening of the extensions . . . every four to six weeks," the company states. "After about six months you begin to lose hair permanently along the stress points where the extensions are tied— a condition known in dermatology as permanent **traction alopecia**. We've consulted with thousands of women who made their hair loss much worse by using extensions." It's important to know the risks involved in continual use of extensions, and which application and maintenance methods are most dangerous.

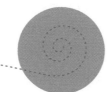

TYPES OF EXTENSIONS

The Extent of the Options

Before we go into the success story of extensions and how they may be able to help, let's look at an overview of the kinds of extensions so that you can begin to consider which may be the best options for your client's circumstances.

Basically, there are two categories of extensions you should know about at this point:

1. Lineal extensions—There are different kinds of extensions that are applied lineally, meaning that they are attached to your existing hair along planned pathways going from side to side along the scalp where needed. They are typically applied using bonding, weaving, or clips:

a. Machine-made wefts—As the name implies, these are constructed strips of material made by machine, so the parameters of what your specialist can do with them are narrow, but he or she can still be creative. Chrissy Vittallo, owner and distributor of the Chrissy V. Extension System and creator of a new cold bond used for applying extensions, says they are effective, but that if you are using them for cosmetic reasons, you would have to double them up since you can only put so much hair on the constructed weft. They are a less expensive option because they are preconstructed without intensive labor on the part of the manufacturer.

b. Mono (eyelash) hand-tied wefts—Although these are strong, the wefts are strand-thin, like hair itself. "These are beautiful wefts that blend in easily in noticeable areas, like above the temples," says Vittallo. These wefts are subtle and may be used for minor supplementation

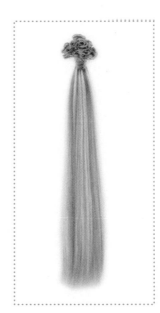

Beautiful Hair—How to Give It Back

of hair, in obvious places, or in conjunction with other extensions and methods.

c. Hand-tied wefts—These wefts can be more expensive since more work goes into them (they are not machine-made), but they can be constructed with greater customization.

d. Ribbon wefts—According to Vittallo, these wefts are best used for hair that is up off the scalp and in more fragile areas, so they are particularly effective when used at the top of the head. The ribbon lies flat, but the extensions add volume and fullness.

e. Polymer wefts—These wefts are particularly good when worn closer to the hairline, and can be attached to the scalp by bonding for the most natural effect.

2. Strand-by-strand extensions—There are three kinds of extensions that are applied strand-by-strand, meaning that a number of strands are applied to an equal number of existing hairs to double them in volume. Typically applied using a heat bond or a cold fusion (except in the case of micro-links), they are:

a. Raw hair—Okyo Sthair, owner and president of New Concepts Hair Goods, Incorporated, and president of Rene of Paris, which distributes machine-made hair products, explains that raw hair extensions come in a wide variety of colors and textures and are usually applied with heat bonding. The specially formulated adhesive bond is carefully placed on the tip of the desired number of strands and, equally carefully, attached to existing hair near, but not at, the point of growth.

b. Pre-tipped—These extensions come with the bonding adhesive preapplied to the end of the section of strands. Robin Knight, a hair extension specialist who often works with these extensions, says they offer a certain convenience and ease of application because the specialist who uses them doesn't have to keep returning to a hotbox (used to apply heat bonding adhesive to the ends of raw hair extensions), which can be messy or can potentially cause mistakes.

c. Micro-links—According to Smith of International Hair Goods, links are applied using a special tube-tracking and clamping process. The extension hair is attached to a cylindrical tube that has open space inside it; your own hair is gently pulled through the cylinder and

Bond. Heat Bond.

Salvatore Megna, founder and president of Mega Hair, which distributes its own extension system, is fed up. "Everyone else in the world is doing it wrong," he says sarcastically. "They're using the wrong adhesive, putting too much on or not enough, and not using the right temperature."

The Mega Hair system uses thermal bonding adhesive, which is a hot melt glue that has been formulated precisely for attaching replacement hair to existing hair. According to Megna, adhesive must reach a certain temperature and water has to be removed from it in order for it to stick. Even though the glue is melted and squeezed tightly against your hair, it doesn't mean it's truly attached to it. When it reaches the right temperature and it's applied to the hair, hair gets hot and moisture is released like steam. The adhesive then reaches its dynamic state. It can be used in three ways:

1. With glue sticks melted inside a hot glue gun, so that as glue is coming out of the gun, you put it on the ends of the new hair, and then attach that glued tip to hair near the scalp; then you return to that spot with a purging tool that heats the hair to "purge" the water.

2. With glue discs heated in what's called a hotbox—a dispenser that takes moisture out of the glue as it's melting down, which saves time

3. With pre-tipped extensions, heating them for attachment

Something else that irks Megna: "It's so important to prepare the hair properly, or the extensions will come out. If you don't use an antibacterial cleansing agent to clean the client's hair before you attach the extensions, bacteria will build up inside the bond," he cautions. "As bacteria grows, it eats away at the bond and it just comes off."

Cold Is Gold

The Chrissy V. Cold Bond is used on human hair extensions and hair replacements, involves no hot pot or glue gun, pins or pliers, and specialists do not need heat to apply or remove them. This is great news for hair, since, as we discussed earlier, heat can be its enemy. The bond comes in a can applicator and can simply be blown on (without a hair dryer) or held for a few seconds to take hold.

A real plus: the bond can be used anywhere. It also comes in a variety of hair-matched colors and clear, and colors can be mixed for accuracy.

The bond can last four to six months, although such long extension wear is not recommended, aesthetically or otherwise. "It's asking a lot of hair to hold extensions for so long, whether they have been woven in or bonded," says hair-health champion Vittallo. "In my experience, any method promising three to six months of extension longevity is almost always guaranteeing damage and hair loss. You will be asking too much of the natural hair, which is already fine and fragile, to keep an attachment and considerably more hair on for a long period of time. Everyday maintenance—such as shampooing, conditioning, combing, brushing, and styling—will strain that attachment. The results become the very reason your client is wearing hair extensions in the first place."

clamped so that the real and extension hair are attached. The good part is that there is no adhesive used, but the cylinder can seem a little bulky and, as it's not flexible, it can be uncomfortable to lie on. Links are better for volume than for length, and you have to have enough hair to cover the cylinders.

Beautiful Hair—How to Give It Back

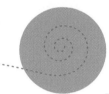

APPLICATION

Extensions are often applied improperly using everything from hot waxes to superglue, which are unhealthy for hair and skin, and a real pain for both you and your client. Most important, the lasting effects of these processes on hair health, fullness, and growth can be tragic. It is extremely important to use the highest quality human hair, use better quality adhesives and safe application methods, and become as masterful as you can at this process.

As I briefly described earlier in this chapter, there are two basic methods of attaching extensions. There is a cold bond, most often used in lineal extension applications, and a heat bond and cold fusion, most often used in strand-by-strand extension applications.

STRAND-BY-STRAND APPLICATION

The Copy and Paste Effect

Of all of the application processes, strand-by-strand is the most popular because it gives the most movement and sway, but it's also the most time consuming and requires the most patience, as it takes about six to eight hours to complete. The strand-by-strand technique emerged both in Italy and California, and it can run your client from $1,000 to $3,000, depending on how many strands are involved.

In a strand-by-strand application, you take a section of raw hair that is 10–25 hairs thick and apply a specially formulated

Profile: .... Tricia

Age: Late-thirties

Cause of hair loss: Stress-induced hormonal shifts

Diffusion Grade: II

Pattern Stage: 4

Face Shape: Oblong

Color Tone: Cool

Recommended Solution: Strand-by-strand extension

Attachment System: Pre-tipped bonding

Lifestyle Consideration: Busy and work-oriented, stressful

Stress is a relative thing. We all lead stressful lives. But Tricia truly had more than her fair share: divorce and custody battles over the children; lawyers' fees; an abusive work environment she couldn't leave because her children's "pre-existing" health issues would not be covered at a new job; two college tuitions to pay; finding a new home that would allow her to keep her thirteen-year-old dog; and her father's heart attack.

Some people would have torn their hair out. Tricia's came out without being touched. She went to a dermatologist, but the treatments did not help. Tricia's hair loss dictated her life, too. She became less social and more inhibited. She wouldn't go on vacation. She didn't swim, go out in humid weather, or venture out when it was raining or snowing. All those weather conditions ruined the work she did to try to make her hair look fuller.

She started to wear dark, solid colors because they made her hair look thicker, and she wore more turtlenecks to detract attention from her hair. A stylist at a local salon in Cleveland, Ohio, turned her life around, however. She noticed Tricia's thinning hair, and recommended that she visit a specialist. When Tricia first walked into the center with her shopping bag full of products, collected from every salon, mail order catalog, and Internet Web site that she could find, the staff knew they were facing a challenge.

In addition to the thinness of her hair, she had another issue. No matter how hard she tried to give her remaining hair some lift, its thinness made it very flyaway and its static electricity made it impossible for Tricia to style. She said that she was just ready to give up and buy a wig, because she simply couldn't deal with the thinness of her hair anymore. She was told it wasn't an option: the last thing she should be doing was to stuff her remaining hair under a wig that might damage the fragile hair that remained.

> "The more stressed I got, the more hair I lost."

After talking with Tricia at length, her specialist analyzed her situation and began to prescribe a series of treatments and styling options that would restore her well being and provide her with beautiful hair. She was shown a video that demonstrated different alternatives and she discussed what her options were. She was amazed. She said she originally thought she only had three choices: accept the fact that she was going to look like she had no hair; get a wig that would look phony; or actually consider taking her own life.

"The consultation gave me hope. I left that day feeling encouraged for the first time in months." The first option Tricia tried was extensions, long wefts of human hair that were bonded in place with a special hair adhesive. "I was going to my 25th high school reunion and I needed a quick fix," explains Tricia. The extensions worked—and were a big success at the reunion.

bonding adhesive to its roots. The section is then attached to a section of your client's own hair that contains the same number of hairs, close to, but not at, the growth point. The bonding is secured by controlled heat under your close supervision to ensure that the existing hair and scalp are not compromised in the process. After the bond cools, it is completly secure.

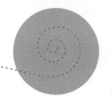

BEHIND THE SCENES STYLING AND STRATEGY

After examining Tricia's hair and testing the strength of her hair, and to give her a solution quickly enough to get her to her reunion, strand-by-strand extensions and a light-density microbond were selected, rather than heavier bonds that would have put too much stress on her hair. Her specialist put 300 to 400 bonds throughout her entire head of hair and her thinning bangs area, and that gave her back her hair in all its volume and length, and gave her the deeper, warmer color scheme she and her team had selected. It was then recommended that she return for a regular check-up to observe how the strand-by-strand bonds were affecting and responding to the hair on her head.

Of the available extensions, strand-by-strand extensions were selected because Tricia wasn't looking for much more length. Instead, what she really wanted was the color, the volume, and the flowing-rather-than-flyaway effect. In addition, because the professionals needed to go closer to the top of the head, where lineal extensions would have limited them, they were able to place the strand-by-strand extensions close to the bangs and in the part area as well. Because her hair was not in ideal condition to color, they were also able to place the already colored strands where they were needed to accent the color of her existing hair.

Strand-by-Strand (Pre-tipped) Step-by-Step Procedure

EXTENSION TOOL LIST

mannequin head	two oz. remover & applicator bottle	consultation form
clamp	selection of hair:	purging tool
water bottle	1. bulk hair	protective shields
comb	2. weft hair	pinchers
wide tooth comb	3. pre-tipped	hair blending board
steel-tip rat tail comb	appropriate cleansing, conditioning, and styling products	remover
loop brush		adhesive applicator gun
tape measure	blow dryer	adhesive sticks
clips	steamer	color ring
cotton rope	plate to use for applying bond to weft	finger protectors
two oz. bond & applicator bottle	design order form	appropriate cleaning, conditioning, and styling products

PRE-TIPPED EXTENSION TOOL LIST

purging tool

purging tool holder

appropriate cleansing, conditioning, and styling products

protective shields (1 package)

color ring

loop brush

pinchers (for removal)

hair blending board/holder

selection of hair: pre-tipped

HOW TO APPLY STRAND-BY-STRAND EXTENSIONS

1. Wash and treat hair as described in Washing and Cleansing.

2. Cut hair if necessary. Make sure it is *thoroughly dry;* blow-dry it with *cold air.*

3. Check if the machine is at the proper frequency or heat temperature.

4. To apply strand-by-strand, follow steps **a** through **h** :

a. Section hair as shown. Make a V-shaped parting using a pointed clip or comb. Hair should be coming directly out of its growth pattern.

b. Center the hair in the middle of the plastic protector shield and secure protector with the clip.

Beautiful Hair—How to Give It Back

c. Holding the client's hair parallel to its natural growth, place the hair in the fold of the bond a half inch away from the scalp.

d. Select a pre-tipped bond.

e. Soften two-thirds of the bond with the client's hair in between the two tips of the application tong until the bond starts to foam or bubble, approximately four seconds.

f. Fold one-third of the heated bond inside; then fold the other one-third part over these, circling the hair with the polymer. Turn this as a whole upside down.

g. Heat once more with the application tong for about five seconds on top of the bond and then two seconds on the bottom of the bond.

h. Once the bond has softened, using fingertips, gently roll the bond from top to bottom until smooth and the top and bottom of the bond are securely closed.

Removing Strand-by-Strand Extensions

1. It takes two weeks for the bonds to set completely. You will experience some difficulty if you try to remove them within this period. Consider using the high frequency heating element, only within this period, to remove the bonds.

2. Wash the client's hair once with the right shampoo and towel off excess water, but leave hair wet.

Beautiful Hair—How to Give It Back

3. If the client has a complete lengthening, we advise you to use the five sections again.

4. Apply several drops of removal on the bonds, one row at a time, always working from the left to right to be consistent.

5. Use the removal tongs and crush the bonds with it. Always use the front of the removal tong. Put some drops of removal on the bonds once more (from the left to the right) and crush the bonds again with the removal tongs.

6. Hold the wisp of the client's own hair with the removal tongs and remove the strand from the hair. Add some drops of removal to the bonds and leave it on for one minute. Afterward, wash the client's hair with an acid-balanced shampoo and towel dry. Next massage the conditioner into the hair, especially where the bonds have been removed. At this point, you will be able to easily remove, with the comb, the natural hair loss and a little tangle by combing downward. Starting at the end of the client's hair, comb to the scalp.

7. Wash the hair again with the correct shampoo. Blow-dry the client's hair with cold air and use the right shampoo so the client's hair is prepared for re-application.

Recommended Pricing Structure for Strand-by-Strand Extensions

The cost of strand-by-strand extensions is based on the following:

- hair cost
- per bond application fee
- cut-in or hair design fee

Definitions:

Service time is approximately 20 strands per hour. (Six to eight hours average for a full head of strand-by-strand extensions.)

Amount of hair required will depend on the client's needs and desires: 50–75 bonds needed to add more fullness to current style, 125–200 bonds needed to add 10–18 inches of length.

With the strand-by-strand bonding technique, the hair is unusable after removal. Clients using this type of bonding system can wash their hair as usual, set and style their hair using hot rollers, curling irons, flat irons, etc., and can even swim with their extensions.

Hair costs: The cost of hair depends on the type of hair selected and amount needed.

Hair price ranges: $50.00 to $500.00

Mark-up: two to five times the cost of hair: based on salon overhead

Application fee: $5.00 per bond

Cut-in or hair design fee: Based on salon charges of hair design doubled

Additional charges: Any chemical processing to growing hair, at salon menu fees. Included in these charges:

1. Preparation of hair
2. Maintenance training

Lineal Application

THE "FALSE EYELASH" TECHNOLOGY

Lineal extensions are the most widely used. Part of the reason is that they only take a couple of hours to apply. The technique itself goes back through the ages to the weaving of the Egyptians. Incredibly, new versions of the technique have emerged in only the last five to eight years. Lineal extensions will run your client about $500 to $2,000, depending on the length and number of extension lines put in.

In a lineal application, a hand-tied or machine-made weft is attached to the existing hair. As briefly described earlier, wefts are strand-thin material, some-times nylon or actual hair, with hair tied or secured to them. Imagining the line that connects a full set of false eyelashes—or the belt section of a grass skirt—will help you imagine how a weft is constructed. The weft is then bonded to existing hairs—near but not at the points of growth—in a straight line going from front to back or side to side. Lineally applied extensions can range from a simple enhance-ment of hair strands to allover additions.

Beautiful Hair—How to Give It Back

Profile: . . . . Kelly

Age: 32

Diffusion Grade: I

Pattern Stage: 3

Cause of hair loss: Post-pregnancy hormonal shift; hair would only grow to a certain length and then would split and break off at the ends.

Recommended Solution: Lineal extensions

Attachment System: Cold bond

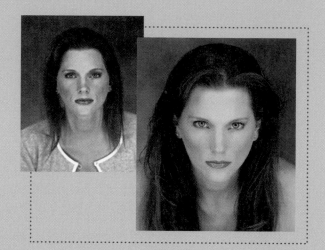

A lot of women can relate to Kelly's situation. After the birth of her daughter, the dancer and former model began having a lot of problems with her hair. To begin with, her hair was extremely fine. Then after the pregnancy, it became even thinner and she began to experience a lot of breakage. Looking in the mirror was so depressing that Kelly began to stay home. She felt so unattractive she wouldn't leave her house. "Every day was a bad hair day," Kelly says.

She and her mother discussed possible solutions. They addressed the possibility of a hairpiece, or something temporary, to compensate for the hair loss, but Kelly thought it might do more harm than good to put something on and take it off every day. Out of desperation, she searched the Internet. Living in Grafton, Ohio, she was not sure there would be anything in her immediate area that would be of any help. And then she found help.

Kelly talked to her hair replacement specialist for an hour-and-a-half at her initial consultation. All the possible solutions available for her were discussed, and hair samples were taken. While she wasn't the best candidate for strand-by-strand extensions, she desired them. Two weeks later, she came in to try them out.

> "Every day was a bad hair day."

But the strand-by-strand extensions put too much stress on her original hair and resulted in a lot of breakage, so lineal extensions were applied to her hair with a fine, hand-tied weft. It was decided to use a light amount of hair to limit the amount of stress on Kelly's original hair, and a lineal bond, which is a cold bond that puts no stress on your own hair while you're sleeping. Lineal bonding also has *elastymer* in it, which creates flexibility and lessens breakage, but which has the ability to hold the weft on securely during activity and in heat and water. Six wefts were used.

Kelly is now happy with her hair, which falls a long way down her back. She can do anything she wants with her hair—she can swim (and even when her hair is wet, no one can see any demarcation where the extensions are), play sports, put it in an up do, leave it down—she can style it anyway she wants. The only thing she has to be careful about is how she parts it, and she can never pull hard on her hair, especially while she's washing or brushing it. Kelly goes back to the salon once a month so that the extensions can be removed, her natural hair washed, and the line reattached. As her own hair grows out, the extensions also move away from her scalp. Her monthly appointments realign them so the appearance is seamless.

Lineal Extensions Step-by-Step Analysis Procedure

LINEAL EXTENSIONS TOOL LIST

mannequin head

t-pins

clamp

water bottle

comb

metal-tip rat tail comb

loop brush

tape measure

clips

cotton rope

two oz. bond and applicator bottle

two oz. remover and applicator bottle

selection of hair:

1. micro hand-tied

2. hand-tied

3. micro machine-tied

4. machine-tied

5. one-eighth inch ribbon hand-tied

6. one-quarter inch ribbon hand-tied

7. polymer wefts hand-tied

appropriate cleansing, conditioning, and styling products

blow dryer

steamer plate to use for applying bond to weft

design order form

cutting and styling tools

Evaluate the condition and texture of the hair extensions and the amount of hair that will be needed to achieve the finished look.

Select color or color combination as well as texture to give balance of color and texture to finished look.

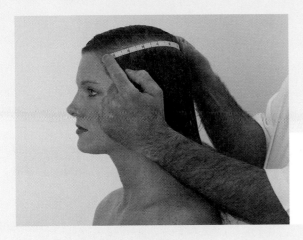

Use a tape measure to measure the total lineal length from the nape to the top of the head; show pattern of measurements.

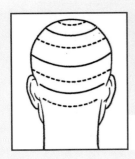

Back

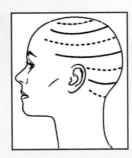

Side

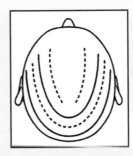

Top

Half head of extensions to lengthen: add some volume; four to five lines

Full head of extensions to lengthen: add volume and fullness; six to nine lines

Select type of weft:

1. Micro hand-tied
2. Hand-tied
3. Micro machine-tied
4. Machine-tied
5. One-eighth-inch ribbon hand-tied
6. One-quarter-inch ribbon hand-tied
7. Polymer wefts hand-tied

Beautiful Hair—How to Give It Back

Preparation of client

1. Shampoo
2. No conditioner on roots; if conditioner is needed for tangles, use from mid-shaft to ends.
3. Dry

Lineal Extensions Step-by-Step Application Procedure

PREPARATION OF THE EXTENSIONS:

1. Shampoo
2. Pre-condition
3. Condition
4. Steam weft to release any wrinkles and bends from manufacturer's packaging.
5. Measure out the planned placement of extension to calculate the amount of lineal length you need.

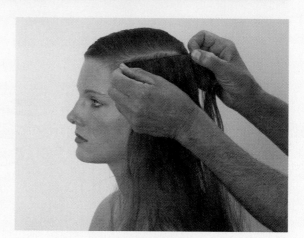

APPLICATION OF HAIR EXTENSIONS:

1. Shake can well. Pour bond into applicator. Apply bond to the weft, then set the weft down on a non-stick surface to allow the bond to set up.

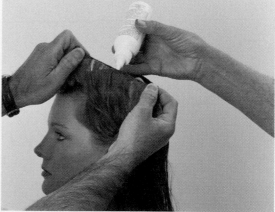

2. Section hair where wefts are to be placed. Start at occipital bone and work upward.
3. Holding applicator horizontally, squeeze a sufficient amount of bond to hair close to scalp and to edge of weft. Dry both areas with a warm dryer for approximately 10 seconds.
4. Press weft to hair, smoothing with thumbs across the weft—back and forth until it adheres. Dry with dryer for approximately 10 seconds.

5. Apply bond to top of weft, then pull a thin section of the client's hair from above the weft down over the weft. Smooth hair on the weft by pressing in a downward motion with metal end of a weaving comb, pressing the bond into the section of hair. Dry with a dryer for approximately 10 seconds. Press again with fingers to assure it has adhered properly.
6. To anchor the corners of the weft, pull a small section of client's hair at the end of the weft diagonally over the corner of the weft, and apply a drop of bond; smooth with the end of metal-tip comb. Dry with dryer.

Removal of Hair Extensions:

1. Squeeze sufficient amount of bond remover on bonded weft and let it absorb.
2. Pull down weft gently, but evenly. It will slide out of client's hair.
3. Spray client's hair with a leave-in conditioner and/or bond remover.
4. Gently brush the remaining bond out of client's hair, using a five- to seven-row bristle brush or comb with cotton. Continue across weft, cleaning weft at the same time . Note: Do not scrape or irritate client's scalp.

General Tips

1. Backcomb or tease the hair and hair spray the area before bonding weft to it. This helps lessen slipping.

Beautiful Hair—How to Give It Back

2. Make sure you work the product into the weft and hair.

3. Be sure the bond is dry enough before tugging on the wefts.

4. Do not attach hair extensions the same day as color.

5. Store all bond, can, and applicator in the refrigerator. Tighten cap on can; the less air in the container, the better the consistency and effectiveness of the product. Evaporation of the solvent will cause the bond to thicken. If it thickens, add a small amount of remover and shake until it is the consistency that you desire.

6. All colors are intermixable; make lighter and darker colors of each color.

7. Clear will turn white after two weeks (quick fixes and bleached hair).

Recommended Pricing Structure for Lineal Extensions

The cost of lineal extensions is based on:

- hair cost
- per line application fee
- cut-in or hair-design fee

Definitions:

- average line = nine-inch wide
- one-half head = four to five lines up to forty-five inches which requires one bundle
- full head = six to ten lines up to ninety inches which requires two bundles

HAIR COSTS:

The cost of a bundle depends on the type of weft and amount needed.

1. Micro hand-tied weft (pre-custom)

2. Machine-tied wefts (pre-custom)

3. Micro machine-tied wefts (pre-custom)

4. Hand-tied wefts (custom)

Hair Price Ranges: $50.00 to $500.00

Mark-up: two to five times the cost of hair, depending on salon overhead.

Application Fee: One-half head = $50.00 per line; Full head = $35.00 per line

Cut-in or Hair-Design Fee: Based on salon charges of hair-design fee doubled.

Additional Charges: Any chemical processing to growing hair, at salon menu fees. Included in these charges:

- Preparation of hair
- Maintenance training

MIXING IT UP A BIT

Now, with the sophistication of strand-by-strand and lineal extension professionals, many specialists are beginning to do both and are combining them for their clients. So you might see a specialist applying lineal extensions on the sides of a client's head and applying strand-by-strand extensions on top, for example. Specialists are finding that they are less limited and that, by using their creativity and insight, they are getting better results from combining techniques. This is an example of why it's good to have diversified skills. Clients are counting on you to have the right experience and outlook, so you can truly make an educated assessment and carry it through.

OVERSTAYING THEIR WELCOME

Lineal extensions, where the hair can be reused, will last about four to eight weeks, depending on the rate of growth of the hair. Strand-by-strand extensions will last four to six months, and then the hair must be replaced. The cost factor or the time factor sometimes keeps women from removing their extensions, which means they put considerable stress on the hair as the added hair continues to, literally, hang around. Those who have hair loss concerns need to consider the state of their existing hair just as much as they consider how to replace hair that's lost. Human hair used for extensions can last and be cosmetically attractive for nine to twelve months with good care, but it would take a truly great hair product and a proper attachment process performed by a knowledgeable and responsible specialist to keep those extensions looking good. It would be foolish not to consider the health of the hair it's attached to.

TIPS FOR APPROPRIATE EXTENSION CHOICES

There are a few overall pieces of advice I have for those who are interested in extensions for their clients, or whose clients are interested in extensions:

1. At the same time you are assessing the health of your client's hair, you should assess her willingness and ability to move forward with extension options. This is going to be

an investment of time, energy, and money on her part, so be sure she has evaluated her investment and intentions properly. If you feel she is going to buy a less expensive, potentially weaker-quality extension that will frustrate her after every shower or activity, then discuss with her the option of buying a clip-on extension and keeping it on for the moment. On the other hand, if you know she is going to make a real investment, work closely with her to determine the correct options for her situation.

2. Evaluate whether she is a candidate for extensions and, if she is, then evaluate which kind of extension would be the most conducive to the condition of her hair and scalp and to her hair's future health. Choose carefully, and take the time to discuss her options with her candidly.

3. Help your client maintain and treat her growing hair. Despite the fact that she has to carefully maintain her new, extended hair, don't let her forget that she has to watch out for the continued health and growth of her existing hair. Otherwise she will increase the risk of losing what she has left, and she won't have anything to attach extensions to in the future. Through the proper use of certain products, and by adhering to a program of care that you will recommend, you can assist your client in successfully safeguarding her extensions and her natural hair simultaneously.

4. Encourage your client to use the proper products. Any time you are working with hair that has been cut off from its source, you must remember that it is no longer getting the

protein and nourishment it would normally receive. You have to use the right products to enable the hair to be nourished. Usually, the hair's outer cuticle has been removed. Normal, attached, growing hair has its cuticle, which is its protective layer that keeps it in good form. There are two hair conditions, depending upon whether or not it still has cuticle. Hair that does not have cuticle is more prone to knotting and tangling.

The difference between the surfaces of cuticle-covered and non-cuticle-covered hair is akin to the difference between the surfaces of silk and denim. That's the comparison. They need vastly different care. Explain this concept to your client. If non-cuticle hair is done-in after a few washes, you are actually the one who suffers, because the client may not understand that you chose a quality product which was conducive to her hair's needs, but which required greater care than she gave it. The use of special products can address that by making sure that the hair is well conditioned and cared for.

5. Tell your client to treat her overall extended hair as though it is a precious, prized possession. She must use the right brush to avoid breakage, splitting, and loosening of the bonds. She should make sure no area of her life or activities cause even the slightest friction on her hair or head. The towel she uses on her hair after a shower or swim should be a shammy. She's going to have to bid farewell to those cotton pillowcases and get satin ones instead. She should cover all the headrests in her home and car, or she should not lean against them. She will have to wear silk scarves over collared clothes made from "rough" fabrics (especially

wool), and any other clothing her hair comes into contact with. The same level of precaution she would use to keep from smudging her makeup is the level of precaution she should use for the care of her hair and extensions. She should be reminded to be wary of heat. She should use a heat-controlled dryer and should not use curling irons or other hot hair appliances without products that contain thermoguards. She will have to make sure that, if she does use a hair iron of any kind, it is heat-controlled and not teflon-coated, which can break or rip hair. Irons should be metal or steel. She will have to incorporate thermoguards and other protective products into her daily routine and mentality. All of these things will have to be consciously practiced until they become second nature to her.

6. Although there is no rule that you have to look for hair that matches your client's own, you will want to if she wants natural-looking extensions. If her ethnic background translates into her hair having specific and noticeable characteristics, try to match her hair extensions to products from that same ethnic source to get the same qualities you would find in her natural hair. If she is Asian, seek Asian hair sources for her extensions. If she is African-American, start your search by looking for hair from the same background. Also, if her hair has been chemically processed, you should seek hair that has been through similar processing. Again, since these characteristics aren't always evident to the untrained eye, your client will rely upon you as the expert for suggestions.

YOUR RESPONSIBILITY

If you need a heart transplant, you go to a doctor who specializes in that and who has the experience to perform such a serious operation. So it only makes sense that your client seeks out an extension specialist that fits the criteria for this particular specialty. She will want to make sure you are certified, and that you have the appropriate credentials and training. If you want to offer extension services, you can utilize a hair replacement center's step-by-step guidelines, or hire someone who has the training.

INTEGRATION

TYPES OF INTEGRATIONS—
Natural Hair and New Hair:
Sublime Partners

If your client does not have enough hair growing on her head, or her hair is too weak for extensions, she may be a good candidate for integrations. Integrations are designed to work in conjunction with, and enhance and complement, your client's natural hair. Whether she has scalp exposure due to female pattern baldness, balding patches caused by **Alopecia Areata** or overall hair thinning due to the aging process, integrations can help solve her hair loss problem.

About 65 percent of women experiencing hair loss fit into a category that can be successfully addressed by integration. If your client

MOST IDEAL FOR:
....
Diffusion Grades I to
II—20–60 percent
hair thinning or loss
Pattern Stages 1–4

Beautiful Hair—How to Give It Back

is losing more hair in some places than in others on her scalp, but still has solid areas of healthy hair in many places on her scalp, this solution may be for her. If she has lost a lot of hair near the top of her head, where extensions would be more obvious in thinning conditions, then integration would definitely be a good method to try. In many cases, extensions and integrations may be combined for the best possible outcome.

THE BEST OF BOTH WORLDS

Varied levels of hair loss on one scalp present a mix of conditions. Integration incorporates many answers to those conditions in one solution. With integration, you can fill in more in certain areas and less in other areas, allowing for healthy hair to be blended with integrated hair. When all of that comes together, it's as though all of the thinned out areas have returned to a normal state of fullness and natural hair is also plainly visible—with no noticeable difference or division between your client's natural hair and the hair you are integrating. Thus, it makes for an ideal appearance. Integrations allow you to add back the 20 to 30 percent of hair your client may have lost in certain places on her scalp, and the 40 to 60 percent of hair she may have lost in other places on her scalp, and still enjoy and show off the great hair she has naturally.

Integrations are essentially fabric or simulated skin that have replacement hair attached to them that also serves to hide the material, and that allow you to bring through your client's own hair. Integrations can be daily- or extended-wear, just as other replacement systems can be.

You might think of an integration as a kind of web—or tic-tac-toe board—of extensions strategically placed where your client needs them. Integrations may be woven in, attached with clips, combs, adhesive tape, or solution, or even fused or bonded to existing hair. According to Darla Smith, director of technical services at International Hair Goods, some can also be affixed with snaps, Velcro, or eye loops, which are used to tie the edges of the system to your client's existing hair.

Ultimately, after the integration is attached to the head so that it stays securely fastened, it becomes a supplemental part of your client's own head of hair. Her hair and the new hair are styled together in the end, resulting in a full head of hair.

Integrations add hair, but only where it has been lost or is needed, to give the look and feel of a full head of hair without covering up or sacrificing healthy, existing hair. And since integration systems incorporate your client's own hair as part of the solution to her hair loss problem, she will feel she has some control over the situation and she will also feel more like herself. Plus, she hasn't had to go so far as to wear what is commonly known as a hairpiece, and she isn't resorting to a wig.

There are five basic types of integration systems you and your client can choose from. Each is made of different materials that leave as much room as possible for natural hair to come through. Here are your integration options:

Machine-made: These integrations are made up of wefts of hair sewn together by machine. Because they are machine-made, they may be less expensive (depending on the hair and materials selected), but they may also be a little heavier and perhaps less natural-looking than other alternatives.

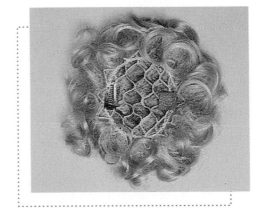

Beautiful Hair—How to Give It Back

Thread (mono thread): These are made with threads that have hair tied to them. The hair tied to these threads has a tendency to slide back and forth, which causes less stability. It is one of the more fragile systems, as thread is thin, and it is only designed to supplement a small amount of hair lost. The thread can be made of polyester or nylon, and both are less structured and offer less longevity than other options.

Cable: These systems are made of cables comprised of three nylon lines braided together, to which the hair you are going to integrate is then attached. As with all your integration options, spaces are configured in the design for natural hair to be pulled through and blended with the integrated hair. Some cables are thin, but some are heavy and can at times give the wearer a "wiggy" feeling.

Ribbon wefts: These are made with a very fine, but strong, nylon in one-quarter-inch to one-eighth-inch ribbons that configure a structure of openings for natural hair to be pulled through. They are transparent or color-coordinated to the hair that is attached to them in order to look like a healthy scalp and hair condition. When hair is sewn to these ribbons, the ribbons completely vanish because they are made to produce a seamless effect, and even feel natural to the touch. This type of integration offers the most natural look and the most secure fit, with the least possible stress on and hindrance of natural, growing hair.

Polymer wefts: These systems are made with polymer, or what is very often referred to in the industry as polyurethane skin or "skin," which is a combination of adhesives and resins, closely simulating scalp skin. According to Dawn Harrison, president of Invisible Hair, which produces integrations made with polyurethane skin (as well as extension strips), when skin is colored to match scalp tone, it also appears more natural than when fibers are tinted to match in other types of systems. Of the five basic kinds of integration systems, one works for simple supplementation and another is used for greater coverage. Thread and cable systems tend to cover about two-thirds of the head, and work best for those with less than 20 percent hair loss and those who want to extend the volume and length of their own hair. Ribbon systems are custom-made in a variety of sizes suiting the varied needs of women experiencing 20 to 60 percent hair loss.

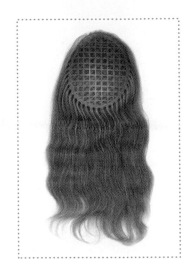

CREATING AN INTEGRATION

Architects of Restoration

Creating an integration that's right for your client's needs is a challenge you should welcome. You will have enough information after reading this book to evaluate your client's needs carefully and listen closely to what she wants out of her integration. Every factor is attended to in finding the optimal materials to be used and the perfect way to combine them to suit her specific needs. The process, from start to finish, involves a blueprint—similar to those drawn up by architects—to help map out her integration so the result surpasses her expectations. Just as there are architects who would fall all over themselves to build the perfect home if commissioned to do so, there are enthusiastic architects for hair restoration systems too, and where integration systems come into play, there are special needs and design approaches that have to be carefully weighed. You should be one of these enthusiastic architects, and you should be aware of these special needs and approaches.

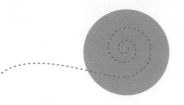

NAVIGATING THE MAP TO YOUR CLIENT'S DESTINATION

When creating an integration, first analyze the measurements of the areas of the scalp with hair loss and take into consideration the areas in which there is still healthy hair. In other words, assess the grade of hair diffusion and stage of hair loss. Make a blueprint, or a map, by using the client's head as a guide. This blueprint will ultimately serve as the design for the integration, showing where to place material with new hair, how wide and where the openings should be for the client's natural hair, and where to attach the system for the best fit, security, and non-detection.

To create the "map," place a transparent film material (see box on the next page) over the scalp and mark it up. Check to make sure the contour of the blueprint fits well on the scalp, so it acts like a mold for the final product. Take design-style elements into account, such as where the part will go and the direction of the hair flow. All of these factors are expressed in writing on the map, and then the map is used to start the process of making the client's integration system.

At the same time, you can fill out a design order form, charting the specific elements that will go into the client's design.

From the map template, configure the matrix, with its different-sized openings, to be made out of different kinds of

The Design Template for Integration

The idea in making the blueprint, or map, is to basically copy as closely as you can the contour and shape of the head so that the integration will fit like a glove. The mold you'll use to make an impression of the head, and to begin designing the integration, can be made of various materials.

A *tape mold* can be made with a clear plastic wrap and tape, or with clear wrap that has strapping or fiberglass tape. A *plaster mold* can also be created, using clear wrap with plaster strips over it. Or, a plastic splinting material can be used to make a *splinting mold*. The material, in this case, is first placed in warm water so that it becomes transparent and flexible, and then it hardens like wax to the shape of the head. A *fiberglass mold* can also be made, using the same kind of material you might see in a fiberglass cast on someone's limb. The fiberglass webbing is also heated and hardens to take on the shape of the head. This system uses a high-tech, medically safe molding material that offers memory ability and excellent duplication of detail. It becomes transparent when soft, providing a helpful cue that it is ready to mold. As it cools, it becomes opaque in color and hard to the touch. It does not require any lubrication of the scalp or any other preparation. The molding materials are safe and medically approved. This is the most accurate mold possible.

If your client doesn't want to sit for a mold, you can try on some of the roughly 20 versions of *fitting caps* that are manufactured with different scalp and hair needs and shapes in mind, to see if any of them would work well in beginning her integration product. Each of these has different measurements and fitting properties. Ultimately, you should be able to evaluate which method might be best for both of you to work with, based on your client's circumstances and the materials available.

material. As mentioned above, new hair will be tied to the material while, wherever there are openings, natural hair will be brought through to be visible. You can begin to imagine how this matrix will have some large openings where your client has her own healthy hair; the material surrounding it will be either widely or narrowly spaced (see above), creating a web effect or something like a tic-tac-toe board, with the material being placed wherever hair is needed. Your client's hair becomes the Xs and the Os that fill in the board.

Next select the color and texture of new hair that will be tied to the matrix and tie the new hair in. When the entire product is constructed, that product is called an integration system. Place the integration on the client's head and bring her natural hair through all the existing holes by softly brushing across the openings to draw the growing hair through the integration system. Then cut and style all of the hair together for a uniform appearance. The result is a full head of hair.

RAW MATERIALS

The type of hair you and your client select depends largely on her lifestyle and environment.

If your client lives in a very hot climate or indulges in a lot of activity, synthetic hair will not perform well for her. Easy-maintenance synthetic or man-made hair is usually the most successful hair to use in integration systems. Man-made includes cyberhair, which is lightweight, has memory, is colorfast, and contains all the pluses of human hair and synthetic hair. Human hair is optimal because it matches the hair it is integrating into. Cyberhair takes shape and holds the style. Cyberhair also holds its texture and shape for the life of the integration system, whereas synthetic hair has to be reworked every couple of months.

PROS AND CONS

The biggest "pro" of using an integration is that you can incorporate your client's own hair into it so that it's not covered up and looks and feels more natural than a full head covering. The "cons" include potential stress on existing hair to which it's attached, and potential skin conditions that may result from extended wear, unless the scalp is properly cared for in the process.

APPLICATION

The size and location of the integration, your client's activity level, and whether or not she wants to remove it at night or keep it on for the long haul determine which type of attachment, or combination, you will use. Clips and combs offer the option of daily wear. But in using clips, you have to be careful not to break or damage existing hair. A safe elastymer bond, such as those described in the discussion of extensions, can be used to apply different kinds of integrations in extended-wear use. There are various types of bonds that can be used. To find the right one for your client, a patch test is recommended.

Making a decision to use one type of attachment system over another is usually based on the amount of hair loss and the location and size of the integration system. You might have to combine methods of attachment, so you should help your client understand what her needs and options are.

TIPS FOR SUCCESSFUL INTEGRATION CARE

Depending on how they are worn, integrations that are taken off at night last much longer than those worn around-the-clock. Well-made integrations can last anywhere from nine to eighteen months, depending on how your client cares for them, the type of hair used in the integration (for example, synthetic or human), and whether they are daily- or extended-wear.

While the new integrated hair blends right in when you first apply it, the new hair and your client's own hair can change color and lose luster with exposure to the environment. If you've selected human hair, which has the most natural effect and lasts the longest, color may be compromised; if you've chosen a synthetic option, the hair may fade. Synthetic hair cannot be colored, and there are limitations in terms of what can be done to resurrect it. All integrations should be brought back to the salon where they were purchased for periodic cleaning, reconditioning, and cuticle treatments. Cuticle treatments, which should be done every six months or so, help the hair retain shine, lively texture, and manageability.

Those who have extended-wear integrations need to return to the salon every four to six weeks to have the integration professionally reconditioned, repigmented if necessary, and reattached to the head, and to care for their growing hair and scalp. To condition, cut static, and generally prolong the life of the integration, your client should be encouraged to use specially formulated conditioners after washing. Some conditioners are designed to be sprayed onto the integration's hair between washings. For integrations with longer hair, spray-on conditioners are a must as they keep the hair from matting and tangling.

The Second Skin: A Look at Polyurethane Skin Integration

Invisible Hair's president Dawn Harrison explains that skin integrations, like the Invisible Hair integration, stretch slightly to fit the wearer and are applied using a medical hair adhesive—a non-damaging, waterproof grafting solution that is strong and secure. The adhesive solution attaches the simulated skin to your client's own around the perimeter of the system only. The fit afforded is reminiscent of a latex glove to a hand, and the skin material is nearly sheer, like a clear Band-Aid. Each replacement hair has been implanted into the "skin" one at a time for the most natural effect.

"This is for the woman who wants to wear her integration 24/7 and doesn't want it to wobble or shift," says Harrison. "She wants to maintain discretion while remaining active. She also doesn't want an integration that is woven in, which may cause a 'speed bump' effect that keeps her from being able to run her hands through it, or that can mean the integration grows away from the head as the hair it's woven to grows out."

The tools your client uses at home are important, too. Air-drying is best for an integration, but if a blow dryer must be used, it should be set at the lowest heat setting, or a controlled-heat appliance should be used. For combing and styling, wide-tooth combs and rounded-tipped or looped-tip brushes work best. All comb through the hair without undue dragging or friction.

And finally, encourage your client who is wearing her integration daily to buy two similar integration systems. First, it's a good idea to give an integration a short break now and then to extend its useful life. And second, of course, if your client has two integrations, then she always has an extra one in case of an emergency. If she alternates two integrations, then she will get the best look and condition at all times.

Profile: ....Mary

Age: Mid-fifties

Cause of hair loss: Post-pregnancy
   hormonal shifts

Diffusion Grade: II

Pattern Stage: 2

Face Shape: Oval

Color Tone: Warm

Recommended Solution: Integration
   System, top of the head, matrix of one-
   eighth-inch silk ribbon with one-inch
   openings with human hair that allow
   her to blend her own hair in with the
   new hair

Attachment System: Daily-wear; five micro clips at edge of underbody of system

Lifestyle Consideration: Very active, no-fuss, needs confidence of secure system

"When I was a young girl, I had a full head of hair, so much so that I used to think it would be nice to have less hair," remembers Mary. "Hairstylists always had to thin it out."

Then she had three children in quick succession—and began to notice that her hair was getting thinner on top. Thinning hair made her feel that she looked a lot older than her 28 years, and it kept her from going out. "It didn't matter how pretty I was or what clothes I wore," recalls Mary. "The fact that I had so little hair made me look old."

Her first solution was to visit a department store and buy a wiglet. "At the rate I was losing my hair, I thought I wouldn't have any left by the time I was 38," said Mary. She never lost all her hair, but she did have female pattern baldness, and she continued purchasing hairpieces at department stores and having them dyed to match her own hair color. One challenge she had with them was that hair stylists weren't quite sure how to cut her hair to blend with them. Another challenge was windy weather, which could flip the hairpiece up and cause much embarrassment. "On blustery days," she says, "I'd venture out only with a scarf on to hold down the sides of the piece!"

Feeling she had no other options, Mary continued buying wiglets for over 20 years, but was continually dismayed, feeling as though she was being held back from living her active lifestyle for fear of losing control over her hairpieces and revealing her problem. When she went to see a specialist, she was able to select a daily-wear integration system, relying on clips to secure her integration. She was able to return to living an active life.

When she first got her integration, Mary went to a baseball game—without a scarf—just to see what would happen when the wind blew. Her hair moved naturally. Her integration didn't blow away or lift up to expose the integrations. She came home from the game a changed woman.

Three years ago, Mary became a hospital representative for her specialist's company. As a representative, she talks to head nurses and social workers about many of the things—their looks, their image, their style—that give women the confidence they need to feel good about themselves. And she talks to a lot of women who have medically related hair loss or are cancer patients—women who will lose, are losing, or have lost some or all of their hair due to the chemotherapy used to treat their medical illness. "It's difficult to speak directly with [them] because they don't like to talk about it and tend to keep it secret."

Mary knows about that from her own experience. "I kept my hairpieces a secret from my friends because I didn't feel comfortable talking about them. That changed," she added, "when my self-esteem was restored." Today, Mary leads a support group for Women's Hair Loss and Hair Thinning. "I take off my hair to let group members see what's underneath," she says. "And it truly shows them what a difference a great head of hair can make in your life."

Behind the Scenes Styling and Strategy

Mary had the ideal face shape—oval—and she was skilled at applying makeup. In creating a style for her, it was very important to work with her facial shape and her warm skin tone.

Her specialist gave her a soft, fringed bang that rolled gently back over the crown of her head, and angled the sides of her hair away from her face to give her cheekbones a lift and highlight her eyes. To show off her excellent posture and also give her the versatility to look sleek or natural, he tapered her nape-line hair very short with a razor cut. Finally, he added warm highlights to the integration hair to complement her skin tone.

Integration Step-by-Step Procedure

INTEGRATION TOOL LIST

- mannequin head
- t-pins
- clamp
- water bottle
- comb
- rat tail comb
- loop brush
- blending shears (44/20)
- shears
- razor
- grease pencil or water soluble marker

- colored permanent markers
- saran wrap or contour analysis material
- tape dispenser
- clear tape
- alcohol wipes
- tape measure
- clips
- selection of hair:
  1. machine-made wefts
  2. thread (mono thread)

  3. cable
  4. ribbon wefts
  5. polymer wefts (Optional selections of parts, crowns and hair lines)
- appropriate cleansing, conditioning, and styling products
- blow dryer
- curling iron
- design order form
- cutting and styling tools

1 Front—Establish face shape so hairstyle can be determined.

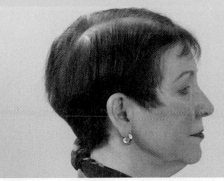

2 Side—Identify the pattern of thinning and stage of hair loss.

3 Back—Identify the pattern of thinning and stage of hair loss. Assess percentage of diffusion.

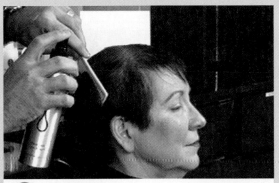

4 Wet hair. Prepare molding template. (See step-by-step procedure.)

5 Mark scalp.

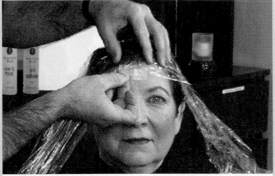

6 Apply saran film.

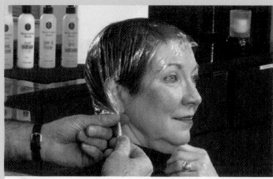

7 Twist under each ear.

8 Hold one side.

9 Hold both sides.

10 Tie under chin.

11 Mark saran film.

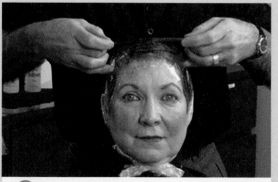

12 Tape from side to side.

SOLUTION 5

13 Tape from front to back.

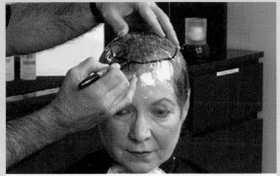

14 Mark outer parameter of saran film, following markings on scalp.

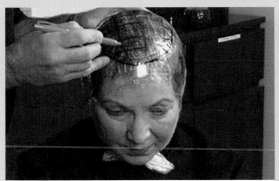

15 Use colored marker to designate material selection and placement.

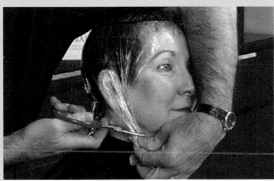

16 Cut saran film under chin.

17 Trim template.

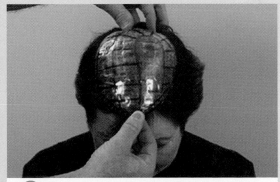

18 Place on head to check contour.

Beautiful Hair—How To Give It Back

19 Mark placement for comb clips.

20 Clean marks from markers off scalp with alcohol wipes.

Measurements

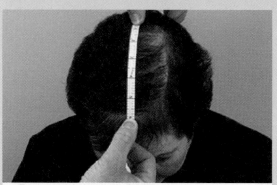

1 Measure front to back (frontal view).

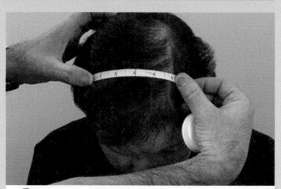

2 Measure side to side in frontal area.

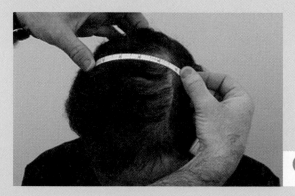

3 Measure crown area side to side.

Design

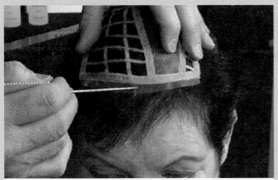

1 Identify hairline.

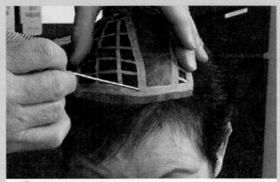

2 Identify frontal.

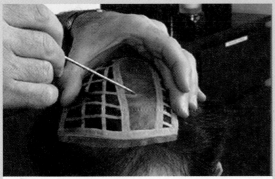

3 Identify design options: Parts left, center, right, crown.

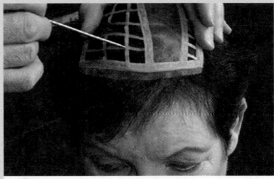

4 Integration ribbon size one-eighth-inch to one-quarter-inch.

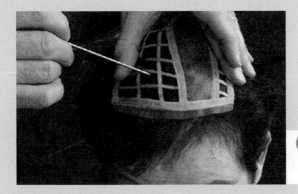

5 Integrate openings range from one-quarter-inch to two-inch openings.

Color

1 Select two to three colors; match base color, mid-level color, and highlight color.

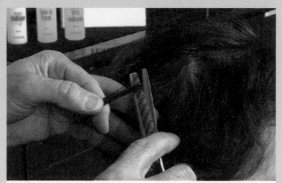

2 Option: Take color samples of growing hair.

Texture

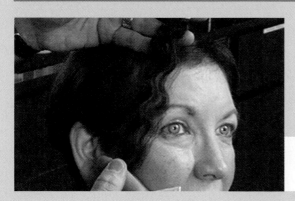

Select wave pattern and texture that best fit style and desired results.

Delivery

① Check all design specifications.

② Place hairpiece on client's head.

③ Secure comb clips to growing hair.

Cutting

① Razor for blending and sculpting hairpiece into growing hair.

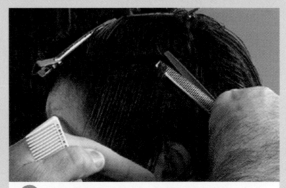

② Blending shears to reduce density.

3 Shears to cut length and layers into hairpiece.

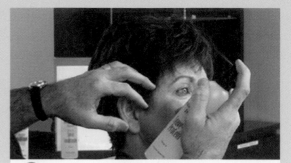

4 Apply recommended styling products. Use hands to style or mold hair. Let dry naturally.

Styling

1 Use recommended heat-controlled blow dryer.

2 Use recommended heat-controlled curling iron to style.

3 Clean and recondition hairpiece with recommended professional products.

Integrations Recommended Pricing Structure

The cost of Integration is based on:

- Hair cost
- Size of construction cost
- Cut-in or hair design fee

Definitions:

- Partial: 0–24"
- Top of head: 25–49"
- Three-quarters of head: 50–80"

Hair costs: Standard length with construction is approximately six inches. An additional charge is added per inch for longer than six inches.

Hair price ranges: The quality of hair selected will determine the price structure.

Construction Costs: Based on design selection and manufacturing costs.

Mark-up: two to five times the cost of goods

Cut-in or hair design fee: Based on salon charges of hair-design fee doubled.

Additional charges:

Any chemical processing or beauty services to the client's growing hair at salon fees. Included in these charges:

- Preparation of hair
- Maintenance training

SOLUTION 6

DUPLICATION

TYPES OF DUPLICATIONS

If your client has no hair (or not enough hair) in some areas to which extensions can be attached, or has no hair to brush through an integration system to combine with new hair additions, you might be wondering what more you can do for her, short of suggesting a wig. There is a solution for her too. If she has more extensive hair loss, you can help her regain the appearance of full, healthy-looking hair through duplication.

The concept is simple. Nowadays, women can make up for a lot of shortcomings. They can use modern fashion or technology to give their breasts a lift, get rid of their wrinkles, and give their teeth an ethereal glow.

If you look at the art world, you'll see that sculptors and painters are often charged with or inspired by the task of duplicating something beautiful onto clay or canvas. This is no small task, as the art of life is a challenge to simulate with a realistic outcome. But these artists have the ability to come close to nature in their work, or even take some artistic license.

MOST IDEAL FOR:

Diffusion Grades III and IV— 60–80 percent thinning or loss

As a hair restoration and replacement specialist, you face similar challenges, and duplication offers you and your client a realistic outcome of beautiful hair, with the potential for some artistic license.

Duplication systems are a step beyond integration systems. In the past, they were known as more advanced integrations, but they now address an area of greater concern to women losing their hair and, thus, they needed their own name. They were dubbed duplications. As you read on, you will see why they are in a category separate from standard integrations.

Duplication systems look completely natural, since they use ultra-thin, skin-like, breathable polymers combined with the finest "silk nylon" to hold hair securely and give it the appearance of flowing naturally from the scalp. Since they are designed to be worn 24 hours a day, they require monthly maintenance.

Duplications are combinations of these nylon and skin-like materials into which human hair has been hand-tied or injected to duplicate actual hair growth on the section of the scalp that is missing hair. The materials used for the base of duplication are more important than those used in integrations because they have to lie on the scalp and look nearly identical to the skin on your client's head. This is made possible by the materials in the foundation of the duplication allowing your client's skin's pigmentation to be visible whenever her hair moves. For example, if the wind blows or she emerges from the pool or shower, the skin that is briefly visible on her scalp looks just like her own. She never exposes any hair loss areas because the duplication looks like her scalp and her hair. As you might surmise, if you don't see the fabric, the duplication lends itself to being a truer duplication of her actual scalp and growing hair. The most important thing for your client to know is that with her duplication, she will have full coverage of only the areas of loss. She won't be brushing any hair through to integrate natural hair into her duplication—there are no holes for even the weak underlying hair to come through. It's called a duplication because it has to duplicate—and improve upon—the scalp and whatever existing hair remains on the head. A duplication can cover a small area of loss or a large one. There are basically three different kinds of duplications you and your client can choose from:

1. *"Skin" (breathable polyurethane or silicone materials)*—This particular design is best suited for the woman who has lost the majority of the top of her hair, and has normal to dry skin; attached for extended wear.

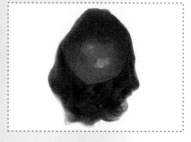

2. *Transparent fabric (nylon or silk)*—This design is best suited for a woman who has normal to oily skin and may have remaining hair, but it is fragile, thin, and not usable in the finished look; attached for daily wear.

3. *Combinations of above*—These designs are best suited for those who have multiple needs and have a combined skin condition ranging from oily to dry. They need a combination of these materials to suit all these varying needs.

Profile: . . . . Marty

Age: 55

Diffusion Grade: III

Pattern Stage: 4

Cause of hair loss: Female pattern, heredity, and medication side-effect

Duplication System: Combination (type 3, as described above)

Attachment Method: Extended wear

Lifestyle Consideration: Active lifestyle, involved in sales, desired to wake up with hair every day of her life with her husband

Marty began to experience hair loss in her early twenties. Until then, she had long beautiful hair, but then she went through a particularly traumatic time during her divorce, and for a time, her soon-to-be ex-husband was still living in the house with her. "He would make fun of me when I started waking up to gobs of hair on my pillow in the morning and empty spaces began to show," she says. "The doctors said it was related to stress, but I never got it back and it only became worse."

> "You never really get over it, so staying involved with support groups and others who are experiencing the same thing helps."

At the time, she tried different hairpieces and even full wigs. She was diagnosed with **Alopecia** and today, has experienced over 75 percent hair loss. She first went to her specialist years ago and they worked on various hairpieces. A year and a half ago, she took advantage of the opportunity to begin wearing a duplication system and woke up the next morning with a full head of hair, which she hadn't seen for many years.

She used to be afraid to go out in the wind, to sit in a dental chair, go swimming, or partake of situations that regularly come up in the day. "I missed having fun with my own grandkids," she says. Now, with her extended-wear duplication, which is on twenty-four hours a day, seven days a week, she can swim, without worrying, and feel comfortable.

She used to wear daily-wear hair systems, but her extended-wear duplication is made so that it looks and feels like her own hair. "It's lightweight," she says. "I can feel the wind blowing through my hair; it's easy to style and to work with, and I can shower with it. The best part is not having to remove it, and not being afraid someone might see what's really going on beneath it."

She maintains her duplication every three to four weeks. "In the summer, your hair grows fast and you are sweating a lot. [At the treatment center], they remove the duplication and clean and condition my scalp with a mask, and then they wash and condition the duplication system. Once that's completed, they re-attach it and adjust its coloring. The whole process takes about an hour and a half. At home, I wash it, condition it, and dry it. I air dry it in the summer because my hair is short."

How did she feel about finally deciding to go ahead with the duplication? "I was apprehensive," Marty says. "It was the unknown, but the excitement of having hair on my head all the time was prevalent."

The custom-ordered duplication took six to eight weeks to receive. "I was called when it came in and we had to spend two hours cutting and styling it," says Marty. "They took their time and made sure it looked as natural as possible."

Then it was on. "I cried with joy when it was first applied, even before styling," Marty recalls. "It felt like I had just grown a whole head of hair. It's hard to describe that feeling because there was very little hair on my head, and it took me back to when I really had hair. I just stood there in awe."

There were more poignant results at home. "Before Christmas my grandkids stay overnight with me. At night, I used to have to take off my old hair system, and the kids would look at me like, 'what happened?' This time, we had a pajama party before bedtime and the kids said, 'It's okay, you can take off your hair.' But I didn't have to take it off."

Marty is an avid camper and she is now remarried. But she met her new husband 11 years ago, during her temporary-hair-system stage. "I was dating him while wearing my integration," she says. "He would say, 'Your hair is so beautiful.' We got so emotionally attached that I felt I had to tell him about my hair loss and accept the consequences. In the past, in other relationships since my divorce, I would tell the men I dated about it and never hear from them again. With my husband, I took off my integration and said, 'I want you to see the real me, because if you can't stand it, then we might as well split up now.' He told me, 'I love you and not your hair.' That was the turning point emotionally—that here was the man who would accept me for who I was."

Profile: .... Nancy

Age: 42
Diffusion Grade: III
Pattern Stage: 3
Cause of hair loss: Hereditary/stress-related life issues
Duplication System: Skin (type 1, as described above)
Attachment Method: Extended wear
Lifestyle Consideration: Needed to restore confidence for business presentations, social
   relationships, and to return to enjoying her active life

"I've had hair loss for years," recalls Nancy, a former assistant systems engineer at a major computer manufacturing company, who is currently a student getting her master's degree. "I'm 46 years old, and early on I noticed that my hair was really thin."

When she was in her thirties, Nancy visited a dermatologist at the Cleveland Clinic. The dermatologist was one of the leading researchers in hair loss for women.

> "I didn't realize how much my hair loss truly impacted me until I found the solution."

"I went through a battery of tests and learned that my condition was hereditary. There was no other cause," says Nancy. The doctor prescribed *Monoxidil,* which Nancy took. She believes it never made enough of a difference to notice. Over the years, her hair continued to get thinner, and she became increasingly self-conscious about it.

"A few years ago, I learned I had high blood pressure and the doctor put me on a prescription that seemed to accelerate my hair loss," continues Nancy. The doctor confirmed that this was one of the side effects of the medication. With the additional hair loss, Nancy retreated from life even more. "I was becoming totally withdrawn. I didn't want to go out at all." Nancy felt people staring at her on elevators and in restaurants. She wouldn't sit at a table where the light was positioned directly over her head. She no longer took pride in giving presentations at her job. Rainy weather put her in a panic. "I only felt comfortable in a baseball cap," says Nancy.

The dermatologist had told Nancy about reputable specialists a few years prior to all this, and she finally went to see them. They outlined several options that would help her. One alternative was a hairpiece with clips. Since Nancy didn't feel very skilled at handling her own hair, she opted not to use the hairpiece, but fortunately, there were several innovative techniques she could choose from. Her specialists recommended a hair and scalp duplication that would attach to the top of her head, an excellent option for women with female pattern baldness, which would make her restored hair look completely natural.

Nancy's new duplication did not come without a little anxiety. "I was nervous that everyone would notice that I now *had* hair," said Nancy. "I didn't want to look like I had a full head of hair after not having much hair at all."

CHAPTER 5

The specialists explained to Nancy that women with hair loss forget that—to the outside world—having hair is normal. People just expect to see other people with hair. So when her acquaintances reacted by simply noting that she looked nice or asking if she had cut or colored her hair, she was pleasantly surprised.

Nancy's husband has noted that she's like a different person—not just a person with hair, but someone who is now enjoying life again. "My own withdrawal was the worst part," states Nancy. "I didn't realize how much it affected me until I had my duplication. Now I go out and I enjoy going out."

Nancy recently contacted a former mentor whom she hadn't seen in many years. Without the duplication, she never would have reached out to this person. She wouldn't have wanted him to see her. "We always say that looks are just superficial and they shouldn't be important, but they are," says Nancy. "Not feeling good about yourself limits what you can do for yourself as well as for others."

CREATING A DUPLICATION: How It Works

Once your client has decided on duplication, a transparent molding template is used to help plot the design of the duplication system. Material parameters for scalp duplication and the array of where new hair will be placed are marked on the template. The template serves as a guide for applying adhesive to the scalp to properly line up the edges of the duplication when it is completed. Duplications can either be adhered to the scalp or bonded, like extensions, to the outer parameter of growing hair. In some cases, a combination can be used to get the most natural look and greatest level of security. Methods chosen depend upon the hair loss issues throughout the area being duplicated.

YOUR RESPONSIBILITY

As the expert specialist, you must know how to execute each step of the process correctly, and be on the lookout for adhesive issues and wrinkling in the material during application. You will also make sure your client's hairline looks natural, know how to style her hair after the duplication is applied, and understand the correct methods for removing her duplication when it's time to maintain it and care for her scalp.

APPLICATION

As with integrations, there are different methods of attachment available, but adhesives are most often used. This is especially true with duplications, because they are designed for women who want to return to an active life with a full head of hair. Someone who is fully committed to a duplication realizes she has a certain level of hair loss and is prepared to duplicate it in a way that is secure. Given that adhesives are a method of choice, you should perform a patch test to evaluate your client's possible reactions to different types of adhesives in order to find the most suitable one for her.

Darla Smith, vice president of technical services at International Hair Goods, says adhesives are the choice of attachment, but that you should make sure you use the best products. In the past, there have been reports of unsafe adhesive methods, such as sealants used for household plumbing leaks and other toxic adhesives, rather than the safer and more secure pharmaceutical-grade products. Consult the MSDS (Material Safety Data Sheets) Index regularly to see a product's status regarding measures of toxicity and safety in general, and use a safe professional grade adhesive. For extended wear, duplications are attached by both adhesive and outer-edge bonding if desired. For daily wear, duplications may be attached by hairclips or combs that lock securely, but that are removable at day's end.

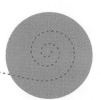

TIPS FOR SUCCESSFUL DUPLICATION MAINTENANCE

In selecting the right duplication system, it's important that you choose the right attachment method with your client so you don't jeopardize her scalp condition and the ability to maintain her natural, growing hair. As with integration systems, it is important for both you and your client to maintain her duplication with care. Her consistent return to the salon to attend to maintenance is key—every three to five weeks for extended wear (depending on personal growth factors and metabolism), and periodically for daily wear, for reconditioning and color.

The importance of maintenance cannot be emphasized enough. Wearing hair on your head that is not yours without removing it for some time is like sleeping in and wearing one particular outfit for that same period of time as though it were a second skin. You really would have to change at some point, because wear and tear on the fabric is inevitable and your skin would begin to need to be exfoliated and refreshed.

Discuss a possible program with your client that would include multiple hair duplications to address the needs of wear and tear and for backup security while doing routine maintenance. See if you can come to an agreement that also includes salon services necessary for a full year of her new look, broken up into 12 monthly payments that are realistic and affordable. After all, you are both making an investment and you both will want the best, most effective outcome.

Duplication Step-by-Step Procedure

DUPLICATION TOOL LIST

PREPARATION:

mannequin head

t-pins

clamp

comb

loop brush

blending shears (44/20)

double face transparent tape

tape shears

grease pencil

cotton balls or cotton pads

template or mold form

adhesive(s) with container

adhesive applicator brushes

proper scalp preparation

cutting and styling tools

REMOVAL:

adhesive remover

cotton rope

cotton balls or cotton pads

cotton swabs

selection of hair:

1. skin

2. transparent fabric (nylon or silk)

3. combination of the above

appropriate cleansing, conditioning, and styling products

Front—establish face shape so hairstyle can be determined.

Evaluation

Side—identify the pattern of thinning and stage of hair loss.

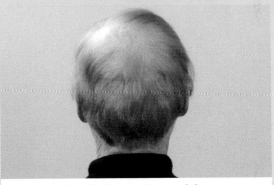

Back—identify the pattern of thinning and stage of hair loss.

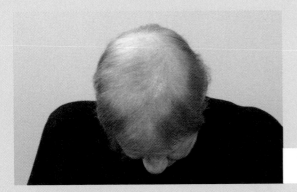

Top—access percentage of diffusion.

Mold

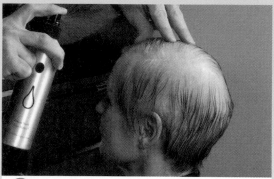

1. Wet hair. Prepare molding template in thermal bath. (See step-by-step procedure.)

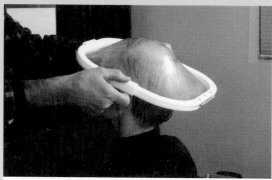

2. Starting at top of head, draw down template to fully conform to head.

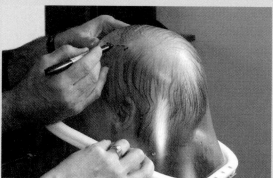

3. Client holds template in place. Mark the molding template for parameter of design.

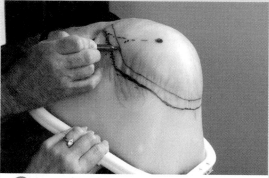

4. Use color marks to designate material selections and hairpiece placement.

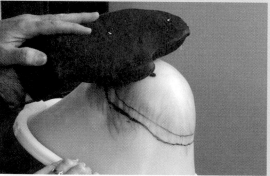

5. Cool molding template with cooling glove.

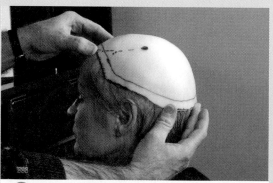

6. With shears, cut along outer parameter. Check contour and pattern.

Delivery

Be sure as in every delivery to review and inspect to ensure the design specifications you have selected and ordered are correct.

Preparing

1 Apply thin layer of adhesive #1 to skin base with applicator; cure until tacky.

2 Place short section of transparent tape around parameter of hairpiece.

3 Overlap each section by one-quarter-inch. With backing left on tape, press to secure.

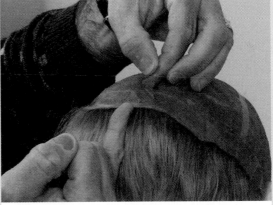

4 When total circumference has been applied, remove red backing.

Beautiful Hair—How to Give It Back

Application

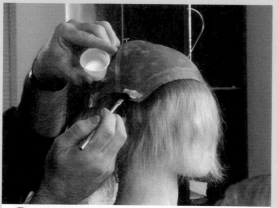

1 Apply thin layer of adhesive #2 to surface of tape. Allow to cure.

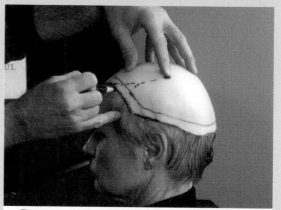

2 Place template on head in proper position. Mark scalp.

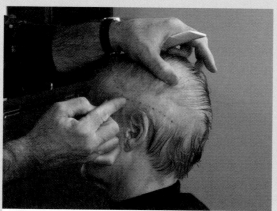

3 Grease-pencil markings give you a guide to place hairpiece.

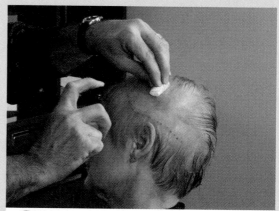

4 Use a skin prep on scalp to protect the area to be secured.

SOLUTION 6

CHAPTER 5

Attaching

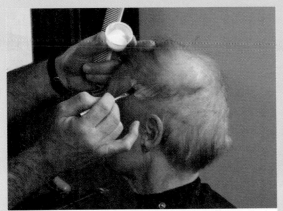

1 Apply a thin layer of adhesive #2 to the scalp above marked area.

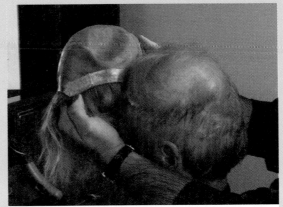

2 Place front of hairpiece on scalp markings. Lay hair line down slowly, matching markings.

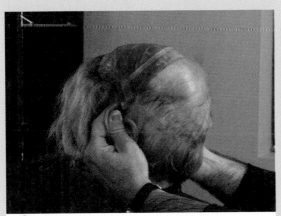

3 Roll back along head, matching hairpiece to markings—avoid wrinkles.

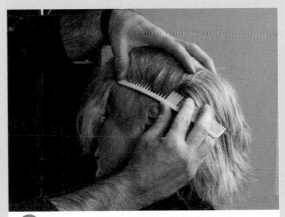

4 Press comb firmly against hairpiece and scalp to secure attachment.

Cutting

1 Razor for blending and sculpting hairpiece into growing hair.

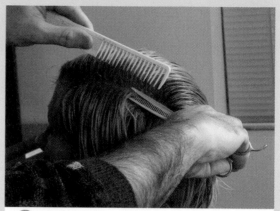

2 Use blending shears to reduce density.

3 Use shears to cut length and layers into hairpiece.

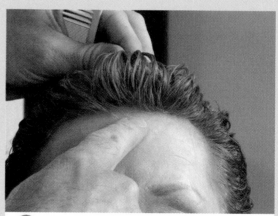

4 Hairline may be too dense. Hair should look as if growing from scalp.

Styling

1 Apply recommended professional styling products to hair. Hand-style/mold and air dry.

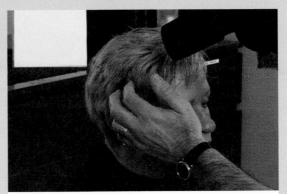

2 Use recommended heat-controlled blow dryer.

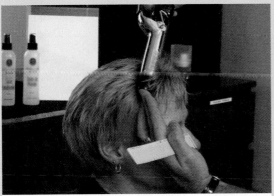

3 Use recommended heat-controlled curling iron.

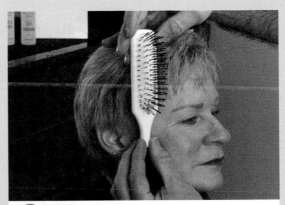

4 Use recommended brush to prevent damage to hair and base.

5 Finish.

Removal

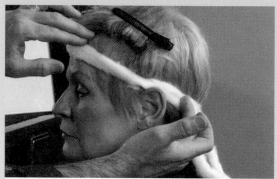

1 Clip hairpiece away from growing hair. Wrap cotton rope around hair.

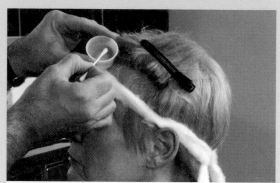

2 Apply ample amount of adhesive remover to edge of hairpiece with cotton swab.

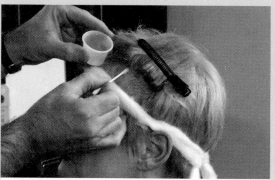

3 Work adhesive remover under hairpiece until it is fully released from head.

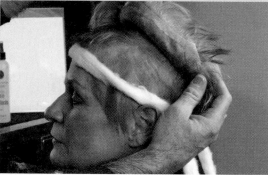

4 Remove hairpiece and tape. Clean with adhesive remover. Prepare for reattachment.

5 Clean and recondition hairpiece with appropriate professional cleansing, conditioning products.

6 Clean scalp fully with adhesive remover.

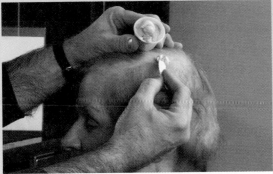

7 Apply mud mask to scalp and surrounding hair where hairpiece has been attached.

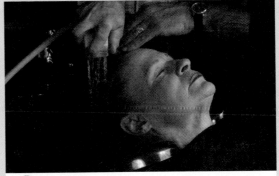

8 Rinse and shampoo mud from hair and scalp until clean.

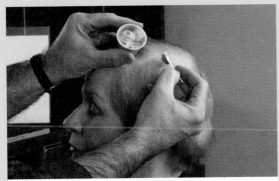

9 Apply exfoliation to scalp and surrounding hair where hairpiece has been attached.

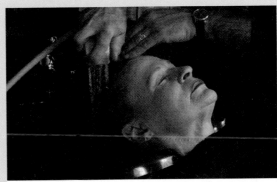

10 Rinse and shampoo exfoliation from hair and scalp until clean.

Duplications

RECOMMENDED PRICING STRUCTURE

The cost of duplication is based on:

- Hair cost
- Size of construction cost
- Cut-in or hair design fee

Definitions:

Partial: 0–24"

Top of head: 25–49"

Three quarters of head: 50–80"

Hair costs: Standard length with construction is approximately six inches. An additional charge is added per inch for longer than six inches.

Hair price ranges: The quality of hair selected will determine the price structure.

Mark-up: Two to five times the cost of goods.

Construction costs: Based on design and manufacturing costs.

Cut-in or hair design fee: Based on salon charges of hair design fee doubled.

Additional Charges:

Any chemical processing or beauty services to the client's growing hair at salon fees. Included in these charges:

- Preparation of hair
- Maintenance training

WIGS AND FULL-CRANIAL PROSTHETICS— Advanced Duplication

INTRODUCTION

We've discussed how you can add hair to your client's own for length and volume and blend partial scalp coverage and new hair with your client's own to supplement her hair. But if your client has dealt with a medical issue—from **Alopecia** to cancer treatment to a burn—that has taken a significant amount of hair away, or if her female pattern hair loss is in an advanced stage, she may not have enough hair to utilize the previous solutions. If you find she doesn't have enough, the next set of options begins here, with a wide variety of wigs and full-cranial prosthetics.

For women experiencing such a great extent of loss, life becomes very difficult. It can't be said any differently. Every experience has changed. Every activity suffers in some way. Relationships alter and falter. Work habits and professional contacts are also affected. But it doesn't have to be this way.

For women experiencing this kind of loss due to medical reasons, perhaps the onset of a disease or the start of medical treatment, this

MOST IDEAL FOR:
....
Diffusion Grade IV—
80–100 percent loss
Pattern Stage 5

Beautiful Hair—How to Give It Back

loss may be abrupt. The psychological and emotional issues that accompany it are acutely different from those that come with earlier stages of loss, or loss and thinning that has happened gradually. There's a lot to grapple with and a lot at stake, and it can feel like the world is crashing down. As the hair replacement specialist, you must understand this.

THE BIG WIGS OF THE PAST

The first fashionable wigs were not designed for women with hair loss concerns. They were offered as solutions for women to turn bad hair days into good ones in the wink of an eye. They were developed for theatrical use or for costuming. They were made to allow a woman to change her look with little effort. But they were never constructed for the needs of a woman who wanted to cover her own head naturally and with the highest degree of security over a long period of time.

Comfort was not a priority. Security was not the focus. Lackluster materials lacked sophistication and authenticity. Final products were devoid of the kind of artistry born of sensitivity.

It may sound like a harsh assessment, but that statement could not have been made if our alternatives today weren't what they are. In contrast, we are fortunate to enjoy the work of companies that take hair loss concerns into consideration when they manufacture their products, and we are lucky to have a movement toward greater education of specialists and stylists in helping to formulate the best wig and prosthetic solutions for women with these specific needs. Comfort and security are among the top priorities. Materials are technologically advanced and look genuine. As a result, final products are artfully constructed and sometimes look even better than your client's own hair would if it were sitting right on top of her head.

In addition, wigs and other products can be made in different ways to accommodate special needs. You can order a wig from existing selections and get it quickly; you can have one custom-made with the ultimate attention paid to your client's specific concerns; or a number of other options in between. There are daily wear and extended wear options too. But before we get into detailing the kinds of wigs and prosthetics available, let's look at how things have altered in the industry to enable these choices.

FAST FORWARD BY MORE THAN A HAIR

Here's just one example of how things have changed: manufacturers are beginning to make more advanced machine-made wigs with nylon material at the top of the head to eliminate the need for a lot of teasing and to take away the crimpy look that is no longer in fashion. New wigs often combine machine-made and hand-tied pieces. They are not as bulky as they once were, since they use less hair, and are not as full and teased. They may still need more attention around the hairline, but they have gotten much better in that area as well. The color, texture, and quality of synthetic hair types are of a higher caliber than they used to be. Now we have amazing processes for human hair that make it stunning when used in a wig or prosthetic, and cyberhair has also changed the picture since its development.

The previous generation of wigs was much poorer in quality than the ones we have today. Yet, with advancement comes increased cost, which is something for your client to bear in mind as she considers the kind of investment she is about to make and what it will mean in her life.

In comparison to integrations and duplications, wigs are obviously geared toward covering more of the head, but usually they are based on machine-made wefts and are less reliant on hand-tied ventilation, although both possibilities are available. Some of the same materials are used in prosthetics and wigs, but not to the same extent.

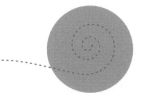

TYPES OF WIGS AND PROSTHETICS

In order to simplify things, let's look once more at the main categories of wigs and prosthetics. *Ready-made* or *machine-made* wigs come from stock and are comprised of a combination of machine-made materials with hand-tied tops. With these, you will have the option of using medium-grade human hair. *Pre-custom* wigs have been hand-tied with synthetic hair. They are prefabricated and come in standard sizes and colors. There are no alterations, except maybe in the cutting after it's selected, which brings it closer to the custom level. *Semi-custom* wigs are hand-tied from the cap system or duplication of pre-custom to specialized needs. When you order these replacements, you select from categories of the manufacturer's selections and have them customized based on your client's needs. You can get these within four to six weeks. Size is determined based upon six to eight specific measurements of the head. *Custom* wigs and prosthetics are particularly good for quickly addressing the concerns of those experiencing loss due to medical

situations. There are three subcategories of custom products to consider: *semi-custom, full-custom,* and *in-house custom.*

It may take 21 to 28 days for a *semi-custom* wig or prosthetic product to be prepared, and up to 10 weeks for a *full-custom* one. For the *semi-custom,* you can fax your client's measurements to the factory, and you won't need to take a mold and cast as you would in preparing for a *full-custom.* Of these two

Beautiful Hair—How to Give It Back

custom types, the *semi-custom* provides you with a greater design selection, but in a timeframe that is more realistic for special needs. A full-cranial prosthetic is an example of the *full-custom* variety. It takes mold and cast work, and the order goes to the manufacturer to be made from scratch. Vacuum-attachment cranial prosthetics would also be examples of *full-custom* products, but they take longer to develop—perhaps three to six months—due to the process, which involves older technology. *In-house custom* products are created completely on the premises (in your salon or center) from the fabric to the blending of the hair. The fabrics are made with silks and polyesters, since you can't heat-form or fabricate with polymers on site, and the process is quite labor-intensive. Turnaround time varies from four to twelve weeks, depending on the scope of production involved.

Certain treatment centers design their own wigs completely from start to finish, and having that customization has proven invaluable to their clients. Like those clients do, your client will want to seek out a specialist who is experienced in developing wig designs and who will work with her to determine how to best suit her needs.

There are also companies that design wigs specifically with hair loss—and medically related hair loss—concerns in mind. Your client may want to begin by looking at some of the styles that are available while she is beginning to consider purchasing a wig, just to gain a better understanding of some of the options.

If your client is interested in buying a short-term product that has a degree of quality, you can look into those made with hand-tied synthetic hair, or a *semi-custom* product. She can use it for six months to a year, and spend less on her investment—perhaps $500–900—until she understands her needs more fully.

Profile: .... Susan

Age: Late forties

Cause of hair loss: Initial thinning, then breast cancer

Diffusion Grade: IV

Pattern Stage: 5

Face Shape: oval

Color Tone: cool

Recommended Solution: Semi-custom, human hair, hand-tied cranial prosthetic

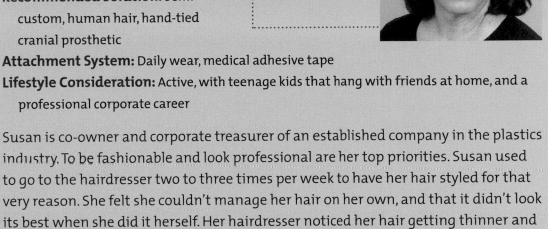

Attachment System: Daily wear, medical adhesive tape

Lifestyle Consideration: Active, with teenage kids that hang with friends at home, and a professional corporate career

Susan is co-owner and corporate treasurer of an established company in the plastics industry. To be fashionable and look professional are her top priorities. Susan used to go to the hairdresser two to three times per week to have her hair styled for that very reason. She felt she couldn't manage her hair on her own, and that it didn't look its best when she did it herself. Her hairdresser noticed her hair getting thinner and recommended she have a consultation with a specialist. "I got an integration which combined my own hair with his product," remembers Susan. She wore the system for six to eight months and loved it.

A short time after that, Susan was diagnosed with breast cancer. After surgery, she began chemotherapy and radiation. Three weeks after her first chemo treatment, her hair started to fall out in bunches. "I asked [my specialist] to shave my head because I didn't want to see the gradual deterioration," she says.

A wig was created for Susan and, from having worked with her in the past, her specialist knew exactly what she would like. "From the moment it was placed on my head, I felt great," says Susan. "I never had great hair and I have gotten more compliments on my wig than I have ever gotten in my whole life. No matter where I go, people compliment me on my hair."

After all she's been through, no one Susan works with knows anything about her health situation or her hair. "I feel good and my appearance has not been affected," she says. "It's made a tremendous difference for me to be able to look like this. Not only did [my specialist] design the wig so it's the right color, but he cut it, shaped it, and designed it into a style that's truly flattering for me. I play softball in it and I do everything in it. I have two teenage kids and they constantly have friends in and out of the house. They are at an age where they are easily embarrassed, and the fact that I wear my hair all day is comforting to them too."

Keeping her situation under wraps helps to eliminate some of her stress too. "It's rather refreshing for me because, since no one knows, no one asks me how I am doing, which would remind me of my illness every day," says Susan. "My philosophy is to look my best every day, participate in the world and be a part of the world, so I can live as normal a life as I can."

Profile: . . . . Ellen

Age: Late 50s
Cause of hair loss: Stress-induced thinning and loss
Diffusion Grade: II
Pattern Stage: 2
Face Shape: Oval
Color Tone: Warm
Recommended Solution: In-house custom, human-hair, hand-tied wig
Attachment System: Daily wear, comb/clips with elastic at nape line

Lifestyle Consideration: Busy owning a difficult business and juggling weekly social engagements; religious requirement to cover hair at top of head; living in heart of urban melting pot

I had started to notice a thinning of my hair on my hairbrush at first, and then on the bathroom floor after I brushed my hair. I saw little balding spots near the hairline. I went to a dermatologist, who examined me and said it was probably stress-related and it was the kind of loss that would stop. He said some would probably grow back, which I later found to be true—some, but not all.

Still, at the time, it became a cyclical problem. It was stressful to me to know that I was so stressed out about my life that my hair was responding by shedding. More shedding ensued. This went on for about a year. I felt devastated as I lost hair, because it is such an important part of who I am. I always had the best hair, the thickest, and the easiest to work with. All of a sudden, with everything else that started changing as I aged, I saw that changing too.

> "I think if you always liked your hair and you had good hair through much of your life, you can't expect less of your wig."

In looking for a solution, I was luckier than some. I had often worn a hat as part of my religious observance, as tradition in my orthodox Jewish community dictates that I cover the top of my head because I am married. I had decided I was not the wig type, as that is seen as more religious than I was ready to be. Instead, I had opted for the more modern alternative of hat-wearing when necessary. But hats fell off sometimes, and I wasn't looking forward to that happening in light of this new challenge with my hair.

I decided to take the step and get a wig—a Shaytel, as it's known in the community—and once I knew I was going to, I knew I wanted to get a human-hair wig. So I went to the place where I thought they would know the most about it—the local wigmakers in the orthodox neighborhood nearby. I took someone with me who had once studied to be a wig stylist and whom I knew would know quality. I wanted human hair, but I didn't need the most expensive. I couldn't imagine myself spending $5,000 on a wig. But I wanted something reasonable and of good quality. I ended up with a natural-looking wig that is comfortable and fashionable. I found that after wearing it for a few months, I needed to revise it to make it more me, especially as my own tastes changed. So, even now, I keep restyling it and coloring it.

One of the most important things I understood, after getting my wig and making sure it was high quality, was that since I had always liked my hair and had good hair, I couldn't expect less from my wig. I think that's important to remember, because if you did have good hair, you are going to realize if this new hair you invested in does not fit the bill or is not good enough. If you didn't know what you were missing, it would be another story.

TYPES OF PROSTHETICS:
The Hair Prosthetic

Full-cranial prosthetics can be daily- or extended-wear, but most women choose daily-wear. There are certain exceptions. A prosthetic is a system that is specially designed with medical hair loss or long-term hair loss in mind. It can be made of a variety of fabrics and materials that will, ideally, closely simulate your client's scalp and the natural look of growing hair from the simulated scalp. It should be comfortable and able to withstand the emissions of the scalp underneath it in order to serve your client over a prolonged time period.

The fit of the prosthetic is extremely important, and special steps are taken to ensure the best fit. Custom cutting, fitting, styling, and coloring are all essential parts of the creation process. Prosthetics are usually lighter weight and more natural looking than most wigs.

According to Darla Smith, vice president of technical services for International Hair Goods, hair prosthetics are fitted with molds and casts of measurements of the head, rather than with simple measurements. These measuring tactics closely resemble those used in creating an integration or duplication. New, carefully selected hair, whether synthetic, human, or cyberhair, is hand-tied to the base material, which can be made of polyester, nylon, polyurethane, or silicone. Hair can also be injected into the base. The prosthetic is designed to closely resemble your client's hair patterns and hairlines, the hair at the nape of her neck and over her ears, and the pigment of the skin on her scalp.

"The prosthetic device allows for confidence in an extended-wear hair replacement that relies on security, and that allows for a more natural lifestyle while wearing it than other options do," says Smith. "You can use a special medical adhesive tape or medical adhesive solution (the same kind used in medicine when securing prosthetic eyes and noses) to set it in place, so the security level is very high."

Full-cranial prosthetics may also be attached relying on a tight fit with the curvature of your client's head, and with adjustments behind her ear with elastic or two-sided medical tape, and even combs—if she has some hair to fasten the combs to. There is also the option of a vacuum-pressure attachment that is made of a hard, soft, or semi-soft polyurethane or silicone, or both combined. Prices will vary due to materials, size and length of hair, and type of hair used. They can run from as low as $1,000 to as high as $5,000, depending on a variety of factors.

For the *vacuum prosthetic,* your client would have to have no hair at all. The lining is stretched over the head, and the prosthetic is fastened to the scalp with suction. There are both pluses and minuses to using this kind of replacement.

"A vacuum base does allow for cuticle hair to be injected into it so you get the beautiful, finished look of real hair," says Smith. "Hair is less processed than it is when the cuticle has been removed, so snarls and tangles are not as common. A vacuum is a very good cranial prosthetic—you are hard-pressed to know what is real and what is not."

But the vacuum option creates security without much breathability, so maintenance of the scalp becomes all the more important. Also, it can be very heavy, since some are made from rubber and polyurethane hard plastic.

"Another drawback is that to make it fit properly, you have to have a perfect head for a perfect fit," says Smith. "And while the people who use it believe in it so much they would never perceive going outside the box, in reality, it's an old technology, as prosthetics have come so much further in recent years."

According to Smith, a vacuum prosthetic can run between $3,000 and $5,000, depending on various factors.

TIPS FOR PROPER WIG AND PROSTHETIC CARE

Your client needs to take precautions with her wig or prosthetic to maintain it carefully. Tell her the following:

- Use special tools to dry it, brush it, and comb it, and keep it away from undue friction.

- Special care must be taken in storing it properly. Keep it on a mannequin head, preferably one made of or covered by a skin-like material, polyurethane or polymer. If you use a Styrofoam mannequin head, it should be thrown out every month because it will build bacteria even when it looks clean. You will need to use a Sea Breeze type of astringent freshener on the undersurface of the scalp base of your wig or prosthetic and on your scalp each time you remove it.

- If you have invested in a vacuum fit prosthetic that has virtually no breathability, you may experience excessive flakiness, rashes, or pruniness. Your body adjusts to this by creating a resistant area of skin, if necessary.

- You will have a high perspiration level and, with that, you will have reduced your best condition for possible new growth. If you are already positive that the growth will not come back, then that's different. Continue to nurture your best opportunity for new growth. If you are an **Alopecia** patient, you may not have that possibility. Talk with your doctor about this.

- The same holds true for you if you wear a wig all the time. Your scalp condition underneath will not be at its optimum level for potential new growth because it is typically encumbered. Also, if you have any growing hair near your hairline, **Alopecia** may develop in this area if you continually wear a wig. You may choose to try some of the alternatives to wearing wigs and prosthetics highlighted in the following two solutions.

- Remember that a (non-vacuum) full-cranial prosthetic is breathable and allows growing hair to thrive.

Full-Cranial Prosthesis and Wig Step-by-Step Procedure

WIG AND FULL-CRANIAL PROSTHETIC TOOLS

Same as combined integration and duplication tool list

Evaluation

Evaluate front view.

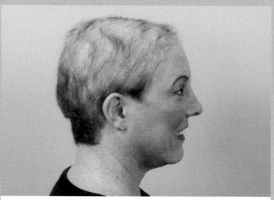

Evaluate side view.

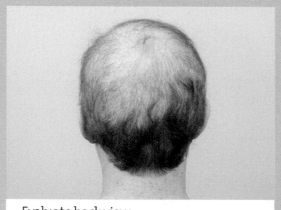

Evaluate back view.

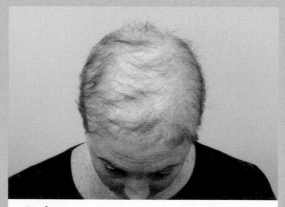

Evaluate top view.

Measurements

(Ready-made only needs circumference measurements.)

Before you start, pin hair as flat and tight as possible before measuring. This will eliminate bulges that distort your head contours.

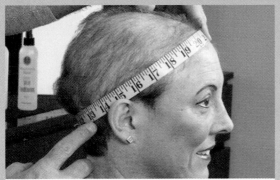

1 The circumference of the head: measure all around head. Rest tape measure where hair starts to grow and follow around nape of neck. Average measurement is 22 inches.

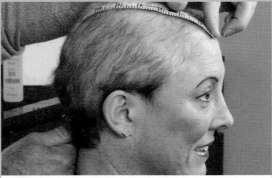

2 From forehead to nape of neck: measure from hair line at center of forehead straight back over crown to center of hair line at nape of neck. Average measurement is 13.5 inches.

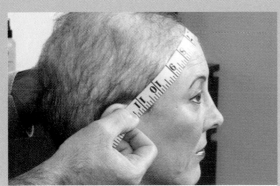

3 Ear to ear across front hair line: measure front of ears, just where hair starts to grow (sideburns) across the hair line on forehead and end in front of edge of other sideburn. Average measurement is 11.5 inches.

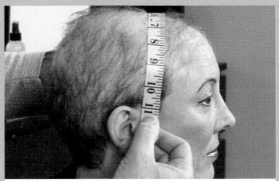

4 From ear to ear over top of head: measure from hair line where hair starts to grow above ear straight across top of head and extend to edge of hairline on other ear. Average measurement is 11 inches.

Beautiful Hair—How to Give It Back

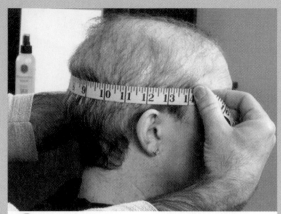 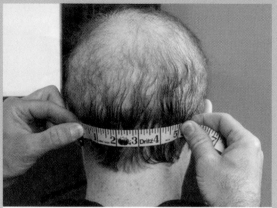

5 Point to point: front temple to temple around back of head. Average measurement is 14 inches.

6 Nape of neck: measure how wide hair grows across nape of neck. Average measurement is 6 inches.

Select type of wig or prosthetic that will meet your client's needs.

Requirements

(See Chapter 4)

- *Ready made:* needs only circumference
- *Pre-custom:* needs only circumference or cap fitting
- *Semi-custom:* needs full head measurements (steps 1–6)
- *Custom:* needs plaster mold. Option: full head measurements (steps 1–6)

Fitting Caps

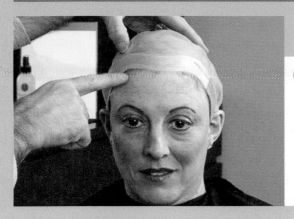

1. After taking the required measurements, select a cap that is the closest to the head size.
2. Check fit of hair line to see if placement matches client's hair line; should be three inches above eyebrows.

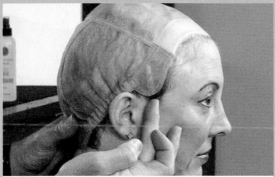

3. Check fit of temple hair line. It should be two fingers behind eyebrows.

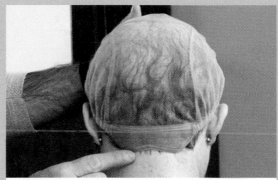

4. Check fit of nape of neck. It should not extend beyond crease in neck when head is drawn back.

Making a Plaster Cast Mold

Step one: Making your preliminary markings. Follow steps one, two, and three as outlined in the procedure for making a frosted tape mold.

Step two: Making your final markings. Then follow step six, making all your markings directly on the CAM (contour analysis material) before applying the plaster strips.

Beautiful Hair—How to Give It Back

Step three: Applying the plaster strips. Measure and cut plaster strips before applying. Working one strip at a time, submerge in warm water and remove excess by running through fingers.

Begin at the center front hair line and encircle the entire head tightly with the plaster strips, leaving at least one-half-inch below the perimeter dots.

Place another plaster strip from front center to back center.

Continue working from front to back, filling in areas to the right and left of the center strip, rubbing with your fingers to smooth edges and overlaps.

Reinforce with side-to-side strips. Dry with a blow dryer.

Step four: Removing the mold. When dry, remove chin strap to loosen CAM. Starting at center back of head, gently loosen mold from your client's head, working your way up to the front. Dry completely, preferably overnight. Remove CAM.

When properly applied, the markings made on the CAM will transfer to your plaster mold. Double check to make sure all your markings are intact and make any adjustments, if necessary.

Design Selection

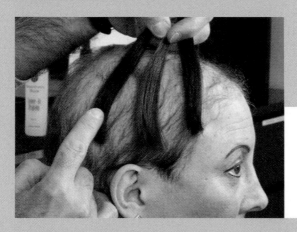

Select from color ring of human or synthetic hair that client has requested for her hairpiece. Match to growing hair or against skin of client for best color and tone.

Select texture and wave pattern that best suits client's desired style.

Select type of wig or full-cranial prosthesis that will suit the client's needs from your consultation with her.

Preparation

T-pin hairpiece to mannequin head about every two inches around the circumference.

Rinse with cool water. Shampoo and condition. See detailed procedure in maintenance section.

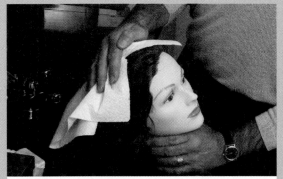

Blot dry and use blow dryer to dry inside of base (not applicable for ready-made wigs).

Apply double-faced medically approved tape. Place tape on designated tape tables.

Remove tape backing.

Placement and Fitting

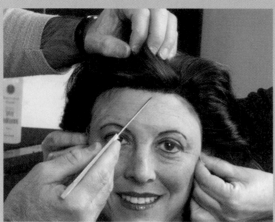

1 Place hairpiece on client's head approximately three fingers above eyebrow.

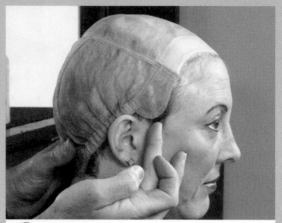

2 Check fit in temple.

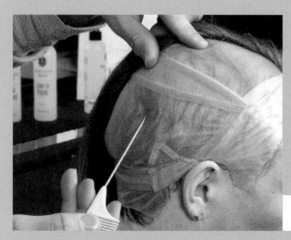

3 Check fit in back for bulk.

Cutting and Styling

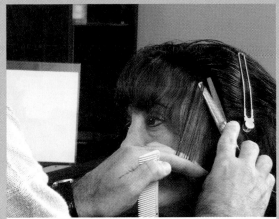

1 Thinning shears can be used at the base of the hair and the shaft to thin and lessen bulkiness.

2 Use your layering techniques. Note: your shears will need to be sharpened regularly so they don't snag or damage hair and fiber.

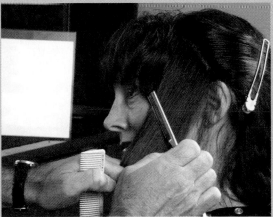

3 Razor should be used when feathering and framing are needed in the style.

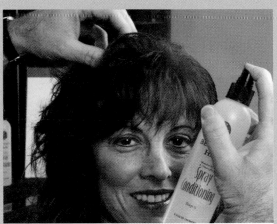

4 Use proper styling products. (See maintenance section.)

Beautiful Hair—How to Give It Back

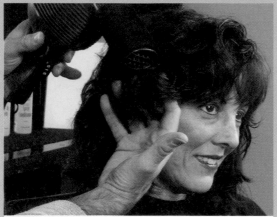

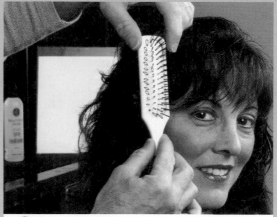

5 Style on client's head or mannequin head using hands to loosen tangles and pre-dry with medium to cool heat.

6 Using recommended loop brush, gently comb hair, and style into form.

7 Finish styling with styling tools best suited for fiber or hair in hairpiece. (See maintenance section.)

Finish

 8 Front view

Recommended Pricing Structure for Wigs and Full-Cranial Prosthetics

The cost of wigs and full-cranial prosthetics is based on:

- Hair cost
- Size of construction cost
- Cut-in or hair design fee

Definitions:

Partial: 0–24"

Top of head: 25–49"

Three-quarters of head: 50–80"

Full head: 81–120"

Beautiful Hair—How to Give It Back

Hair costs: Standard length with construction is approximately six inches. An additional charge is added per inch for longer than six inches.

Hair price ranges: The quality of hair selected will determine the price structure.

Construction costs: Based on design selection and manufacturing costs.

Mark-up: Two to five times the cost of goods.

Cut-in or hair design fee: Based on salon charges of hair design fee doubled.

Additional Charges:

Any chemical processing or beauty services to the client's growing hair at salon fees. Included in these charges:

- Preparation of hair
- Maintenance training

SOLUTION 8

ALTERNATIVES

If your client is not interested in wearing a wig or full-cranial hair prosthetic, but is at a stage in which that kind of complete coverage and security is important to her, she may be among the 10–15 percent of women in this diffusion grade category who opt for a *hair alternative*.

Your client may be any age, but if her hair loss has reached this level, a hair alternative may be helpful. Just as there are wigs for children, there are hair alternatives that will work for them too. And just as there are fun young styles for kids, there are fun and energetic styles for their older sisters.

Hair alternatives are hair fashion accessories that cover the entire head so that no part of the scalp shows. Some of them have hair additions (see solution 9) attached to them and some do not, so they may range from a simple head scarf to a beret with hair streaming out of its parameters. They can be under-stated and low-profile, or they can be very fashionable and make a statement to the world about your client. They can be casual for a run to the supermarket, or designed with very special details for events and occasions where your client will be seen and admired. They come in the form of hats, scarves, snoods, and other items, and in a host of textures, colors, and styles. Many come with hair additions, too, so there's a very wide selection of possibilities. Add to that your ability to work with your client to design hers according to her personal taste! Get ready, because covering your client's

MOST IDEAL FOR:
Diffusion Grade IV—
90–100 percent loss

head has never been so much fun, especially given her ability to frequently alternate her style.

For clients who have suffered from **Alopecia**, or hair loss that was related to lupus, cancer, burns, or other medical issues, a wig or hair alternative may be the best option. A huge number of manufacturers have responded overwhelmingly with wig options to choose from.

However, there are only a handful of mainstream hair alternative manufacturers by comparison. There may be as few as 10 involved in the national market, but the good news is that they were founded by, and are run predominantly by, women who began their missions due to personal experience. Their intimate understanding of the issues has added to their success.

Hair alternatives are made to cover areas that are not normally covered, since hair loss from disease or treatment dictates that hair will be lost from unusual areas—such as directly over the temples, at the nape of the neck, and over the sides of the ears. Two of these areas are not standard areas of loss for most women.

The quality of the hair alternative directly correlates with the manufacturer's understanding of both the problem and the current fashion. The more they know, the better the alternative will be. Often, the more they have experienced, the more they know. This explains the success of many of the women who run these companies.

Hair alternatives have been customized for women who required the utmost in fashion. One client went to her daughter's wedding in a chic chignon that made her look like a tasteful Hollywood star walking the red carpet. She wore a turbanesque hair alternative that had a hair addition attached to it, and the hair at the nape of her neck and near the sides of her turban complemented the beautiful pattern and texture of the turban.

Every detail was attended to with the greatest sensitivity and artistic flair to achieve the look she needed for such a momentous and personal occasion. Customization is key.

Clients are also often pleased with their casual, natural-looking head kerchiefs that have hair attached to them. One young client walked out of a center a dead ringer for a funky skate-chick ready to hang with her buddies, her Gap-style triangular head scarf tied tightly with long hair flowing out of it. A young mother left a treatment center with a sweet hat and lilting curls bouncing off her shoulders. Anything is possible.

ALTERNATIVE ENTREPRENEURS

One of the reasons why anything is possible is that there are women like Isa Lefkowitz. Isa is the founder and president of Isa Designs, a company that designs hair alternatives in the form of snoods (turban-like coverings that are elongated in the back as though covering hair beneath them), hats, scarves, headbands, caps, and even rain hats and after bath turbans. She is one example of a woman who was touched by the effects of disease on hair and turned her life's work into a way to help. She had already begun a career in design, when events in her life turned her attention to the needs of women who were losing their hair.

"I was living in New York, where I attended the Fashion Institute of Technology, and I was volunteering at Mount Sinai Hospital," she says. "A lot of the women I came across in the cancer ward were not only sick, sad, and depressed, they also looked like they were not well because of what they were wearing on their heads after losing their hair. I decided these women needed something that looked natural, covered their hairlines, and felt comfortable—especially since some of them said their scalps hurt as they lost their hair and went through their treatments. My designs have come from the needs of the many women I have spoken with."

Isa's designs don't just drop down over the ear, they drop down in a unique way to the nape of the hairline, and caps are arched in a way that gives the illusion of a natural frontal and side hairline. She experiments with her clients by draping materials and fabrics in her studio to see what will work.

She also adds an element of fun, designing baseball caps and ponytail caps for women to help them take their minds off their disease when they look in the mirror. "Having fun with it is a part of how they can get through this difficult time," Isa says.

The human and synthetic hair used in the hair additions she attaches to her hair alternatives is matched carefully and can be cut by the woman or her stylist later if the woman wants to have it shortened, or if she wants the style changed. Some of the hair alternatives utilize more than one type of alternative material, rather than using an alternative along with an addition. For example, a hair alternative cap may have a scarf hair alternative tied fashionably behind it, simulating the way hair might come forth at that spot.

"I design things on all of my caps based on the needs of the client," says Isa. "One time, I had a girl send me four caps and I added hair on them—the exact same hair on all of them—and she wears them all the time."

Hair alternatives are often designed to be secure on their own, which offers the greatest level of convenience as wearers can simply throw them on and tighten them. But they can also be attached for added security with tied material beneath them, or a daily-wear adhesive tape or solution if necessary.

Isa and other designers like her give professionals in the hair replacement industry more to work with in offering solutions to our clients, and they give the clients greater options for coverage if they aren't completely comfortable with the idea of investing in a wig or prosthetic.

SOLUTION 9

ADDITIONS

There are other products that address hair loss and thinning, some of which may be better for earlier stages and some are for more advanced hair loss. They all fall under a common category: accessories.

Let's look at the kinds of accessories used in earlier stages of thinning and loss—*hair additions*. If you live in a big city, you may have seen some imitations of these being sold by street vendors or small import shops, and if you live near a shopping mall, you've seen them in booths between stores and in accessory chains.

They are products that have synthetic hair attached to them. People are always trying them on and buying them for fun. Some of the hair additions are elastic bands used to bind ponytails or hair from the top of the head that is pulled back and fastened above hair that falls over the shoulders, with other hair closely matched to natural hair. The hair encircles the elastic, so you can produce a full, feathered effect coming out of natural, gathered hair. You can also find alligator clips, banana clips, Scuuncis, hair clips, combs, and headbands with hair coming out of them in all different shades and directions.

In higher-quality versions, hair additions come with a higher grade of replacement hair that looks more genuine. They can be ordered, or made, to see what kinds of supplemental measures your client can take to simply make up for thinning areas or cover one or two areas of loss. They can be used as a way to test what your client likes and what

> ### MOST IDEAL FOR:
> Diffusion Stages I to II—10–50 percent thinning or loss

looks good without too much expense and with little or no consultation with anyone else.

These options have been used for various reasons in other sectors of society—not necessarily in relation to women who are dealing with hair loss issues. In theater, film, and costume arenas, they have proven to be fast, effective ways to change a look. Most of the time, we don't even realize they are being put to this use. Consider Madonna on her Blond Ambition Tour. If you take a good look at her documentary *Truth or Dare*, which chronicles that tour, you will note that her natural hair is about shoulder length at the time of the tour. Yet, during a good portion of her shows, she appears with a tightly placed high-ponytail with a cascading, straight, blonde length of hair suspended from it, the knot of which is encircled by a crown of meticulous braiding. We know she didn't cut and grow her hair throughout her tour schedule, varying her natural length from week to week or even night to night. She may have even used both looks in one show. This was an extremely successful use of a hair addition. It was widely noticed and emulated.

Consider also the starlets of the sixties, whose use of the famous fall of hair allowed them to achieve a raised style just behind the crown and to add fullness and sway to their 'dos. They set the tone for an entire movement of fall-wearing across America and throughout the world.

Robert Anzivino, founder and president of Look of Love, a company that produces professional quality wigs and hair additions, defines hair additions as any fashion accessory that connects to a person's hair, whether it's in the form of banana combs, clips, snap-ons, interlocking wing combs, or others. Anzivino was born into the hair business, with a mother and a brother who had their own salons while he was growing up; he also has had one of his own. But once he got into the hair goods business, he never looked back. He didn't have to—he invented the Pony Express, a banana clip hair attachment widely copied today, and the Butterfly Clip that you pinch to open. He describes other resourceful additions to portray the wide variety of options, like Hair Betweens, which are a series of elastic wefts that go over your hair, then your hair is pulled through them, like instant, mini-integrations.

"There are smaller hair additions for the top of the head, as well as longer, larger products that can be stretched from temple to temple across the top or front, and then be clipped into and hidden by your hair," says Anzivino. While his company, Love International, a top producer of wigs and additions, sells many varieties of wigs, Love claims they sell more hair additions by comparison. This is an indication that, while the market varies in terms of demand, there is considerable focus on how to use hair additions. While hair additions don't act as replacements for thinning hair, they can assist in camouflaging and creating the illusion of more hair, while offering fun alternatives.

SURGICAL PROCEDURES

TRANSPLANTS

Women are investigating surgical solutions all the time, and it's a good thing they are. There are so many possibilities to help women who are losing or have lost hair, and surgery is just another viable option. You might suggest that your client do so if her loss is significant but not complete, and she wants to change her life back permanently.

"The great majority of women with typical female pattern hair loss can be helped significantly," says Dr. Larry L. Bosley of Bosley Medical Hair Restoration. "Though women lose hair in a different pattern than men do—often thinning behind the hairline—the treatment procedures are similar."

There are a few options that can be done surgically to help restore the look of naturally fuller hair. They are hair transplants, laser transplants, scalp reduction, and scalp lifting. Let's look at them one at a time.

MOST IDEAL FOR:
....
those experiencing
Diffusion Grades
III and early IV—
60–85 percent loss

Beautiful Hair—How to Give It Back

HAIR TRANSPLANTS

With transplanting hair in the tissue that cultivated it, your client is taking growing, healthy hair to a spot on her head that doesn't have it and encouraging it to grow and flourish in that spot. One of the most important considerations with regard to women and transplantation is whether or not they will be considered good candidates for transplants. When transplants are done on men, the donor area (from which the transplanted hair and accompanying tissue is taken) is usually at the back of the head, where men least often lose their hair. This batch of hair is genetically programmed not to be susceptible to DHT, the hormone that bonds with hair's molecular structure and causes it to thin and fall out. That's why the hair in that area is great to use for transplants. Even after it is transplanted to an area where hair is usually susceptible to DHT, it still acts as hair that's not, despite its new home. This ability of transplanted hair to act as it did in its old environment, while in an area where loss was inevitable, is called donor dominance. In women, however, this donor area is often a place where hair has thinned or fallen out. It's important to make sure there is enough hair there to use for transplanting, and that it's in a healthy state to provide a new foundation elsewhere.

According to Dr. Bosley, this isn't so difficult. "Women usually have a similar donor area to men. This means they have enough supply to fulfill the demand, so the results are usually very good."

But other specialists say there may be cause for concern. Dr. Matt Leavitt, founder of Medical Hair Restoration, says that the donor hair is the first factor doctors evaluate in determining the candidacy of a woman for transplantation. They examine the donor hair to determine if it is genetically programmed never to be lost. "In women, it's not always a guarantee," Leavitt says.

According to Leavitt, there are other factors to consider when evaluating candidacy. Doctors look at aesthetics such as the color of existing hair. Some colors make it easier to achieve a natural look. They evaluate the age and family history of a patient to determine whether she might lose more hair and how much more she might expect to lose. Doctors also try to understand the patient's expectations to determine whether a procedure will realistically help her achieve the results she wants in areas where she has experienced hair loss. They ask questions about the financial investment the client is prepared to make in order to go through the procedure or a few procedures, and then ask about her willingness to take appropriate care of her new hair as it grows and to take steps to prevent further loss. They don't want the patient to be caught in the middle of treatment without being able to afford the rest, or the result will suffer and the initial investment will have been in vain.

Dr. Leavitt asserts that if a patient has a reasonable area of donor hair to achieve results that are consistent with her expectations, she would probably be a good candidate. "Two-thirds of the women we see are usually good candidates," he says.

When transplants first came on the scene in America, in New York City in the 1950s, doctors used something similar to a round cookie cutter method, and took out a round cylinder of tissue, about six millimeters in diameter, containing around 20 to 40 hairs. They would remove the tissue at the bottom of the hair and place the hair into the area affected by loss. The process worked, but aesthetically, it looked unnatural. There was no direction in the hair growth, and the hair emerged from a smaller, more condensed area.

According to Dr. Leavitt, the old method asked a lot of the body in terms of healing. Also, hair was hard to direct and angle. Getting blood supply to the new tissue around the replaced hair was also a challenge. Plus, the procedure created new styling issues, because the scar at the back of the head, where the hair was taken from, was easy to see.

Luckily, today's tactics work much better. The current trend involves transplanting smaller pieces of tissue, less than a single millimeter in diameter, with one to five hairs per section. The procedure involves such small grafts that it often requires microscopic dissection. The strip of tissue is so thin that it allows doctors to effectively hide the incision and it allows the patient to go back to the same area in the future on the second procedure, if there is one. There are no visible signs in the back of the patient's head.

Technically speaking, when one or two follicular units are grafted, the grafts are so small they are referred to as *micrografts*. Grafts of three to five follicular units make up *minigrafts*. The smaller the graft, the closer it may be placed toward the front of the head, so that the progression of hair is more natural—not suddenly thick toward the front of the hairline.

Other things have changed since the 1950s too. Nowadays, there is more emphasis on making sure the procedure brings forth results that are attractive. Even the best-schooled doctors and specialists admit that there is more artistry in the process than surgery. This is true in particular where the front of the head or the hairline is concerned. Very tiny incisions are made along or above the hairline and small single or double strands are used in order to bring the transplanted grafts as close together as possible.

"In the past," says Dr. Leavitt, "we needed large spaces between them so we didn't compromise blood supply. Now we use a pinprick method, so that even in one session we see natural and even distribution of coverage." Dr. Leavitt says the average section nowadays holds about 1,200–1,500 strands of hair. "We are covering larger areas with natural distribution, following the flow of the naturally growing hair," says Leavitt. And now, instead of creating a wall-of-hair effect that shows obvious, strong hair in a line, doctors are aiming for a more randomized, scattered, natural look, more akin to the early thinning stages, offering up slight imperfection in favor of convincing authenticity.

A main downside in transplantation can be avoided while evaluating the patient's expectations. It's similar to, but more serious than, what happens when clients come in for a haircut and you give them a terrific cut, but it is not what they were expecting. It can swing beautifully and fall wonderfully, but if it's not what they wanted, then they won't be happy with it.

It's the same in surgical hair transplants: if your client has certain expectations and the result of her transplant doesn't meet them, she will not be happy. It won't matter that the transplant is undetectable, or masterfully and artfully done. If it doesn't achieve what she expected, she will feel a good job wasn't done. That's why doctors really evaluate a client's expectations when she comes in so they can understand exactly what she envisions and hopes for. "Sometimes, we slightly downplay our expectations so the client can be more creative in her decision-making about the procedure and be more satisfied in the end, " Dr. Leavitt says.

There are also ethnic considerations in investigating whether or not your client should opt for transplants. There are characteristics of ethnic hair that have to be accommodated, both technically and aesthetically, in transplantation. For example, according to Dr. Leavitt, Asian hair is thicker, and although an Asian woman might have 25 percent less hair than a Caucasian woman, it might appear that she has more due to the larger diameter of her hair. In such a case, Dr. Leavitt says, "we try to angle hair forward after grafting, because the hair transplant would be more visible on this woman's scalp due to the large diameter of her hair." African-American women enjoy a greater curl pattern than most other ethnicities of women. "Technically that may present a greater challenge in harvesting the hair, but if you have an experienced professional doing your transplants, you can cover more area of the surface because of the extensive curl pattern," says Dr. Leavitt. "In addition, you can cover thinning spots well because there is less of a color pigmentation gap between the hair and the scalp among African-American women than among many other ethnicities of women."

Another problem that may be faced in transplantation is that when a transplant is performed, the patient may have hair on her head that exists in stages of near loss, and that loss may be accelerated during surgery. During miniaturization, hair that is shrinking is very susceptible to loss, particularly when sudden change occurs. Although new surgical processes are less "shocking" to the hair than the old ones were, doctors sometimes see stress take its toll on already miniaturized hair, so they witness what they call "shock loss" near where they graft.

Finally, some women who have progressed to a certain extent of hair loss by the time they come in for their consultation have lost hair that would have been good for transplanting. Some will have additional loss later in life, which makes them difficult candidates now. To understand this better, imagine you had hair transplanted to a new area of your head, and then a few years later you lose hair around the new hair and also hair that could be used for future transplanting. It may become like a game of checkers, leaving blank spaces behind and making moves all over the board as time goes on.

LASER TRANSPLANTS

Lasers have infiltrated the surgical arena, and it seems people are putting themselves under laser light for all types of correctional procedures. Transplants can also be achieved with laser surgery, but the technique is controversial because many specialists believe that laser incisions are bad for the health of growing hair.

"There's a tremendous amount of marketing going on right now in the hair replacement field, and a lot of doctors are making a fancy name for their procedure in order to get business," quips Dr. Leavitt. "When we talk about lasers in hair transplantation, I think it's more a marketing thing. Heat used in laser surgery can cause problems for nearby hair." Dr. Leavitt says that lasers may have become better over the years, making heat dissemination much less of an issue. "But," he says, "I am not convinced that we have a laser today that is performing as well as other techniques."

Dr. Leavitt is not alone in his concerns. According to information provided by Coastal Medical Group, which conducts laser hair transplants in Tampa, Florida, older lasers used in surgery caused damage to local blood supply and could have caused heat damage too. But newer lasers, like the Erbium (cold-ablating) laser, which they use, maintain the blood supply so transplanted grafts survive more often. The company also states that the Erbium laser takes away tissue that has completely lost hair as it prepares skin to receive new grafting, and that the laser practically eliminates the possibility of infection. While controversial, laser transplantation is still an option.

"In laser transplantation, we harvest hair conventionally with a scalpel," says Dr. Paul Riggs, clinic director of the Coastal Medical Group. "We take a unit of hair follicles that mimics what we're born with. The laser creates a tiny hole in the receiving area and allows us to puts the grafts closer together," he says. "Also, in non-laser transplantation, you are spreading apart the tissue that has no hair, and the grafting sometimes puts pressure on the tissue that causes the transplanted hair grafts to pop out. The laser removes hairless tissue, which allows you to put the grafts closer together more securely."

Riggs addresses some of the transplantation professional's concerns as well. "Some feel that when the laser burns a hole in the tissue, it ruins blood supply to the tissue and the follicles it supports, but that is characteristic of the older CO_2 lasers that were used," Riggs says. "We use the Erbium laser, which has an affinity for water—a main component of our skin—so there is no disruption of blood supply and no scarring. The Erbium is also faster than the old laser. It is an ablating laser, which means it instantaneously removes bald tissue."

Dr. Riggs is quick to add that laser transplantation is not the sole answer, and that other methods may accomplish what the patient is looking for. "It's not the only way to go, but it's a good alternative," he says. "My advice to those who are looking into transplants is to remember that this is a cutthroat industry, so beware of those surgeons who bad-mouth others in promoting their own methods." Dr. Riggs encourages potential patients to investigate their options and use their powers of discernment after educating themselves.

According to Dr. Riggs, Erbium laser transplantation was used for many years in Europe, and after the Food and Drug Administration approved it here in 1997, his was the first clinic to use it commercially. His clinic can do a transplantation procedure, on average, in three to four hours, and charges about four dollars per graft. A procedure for the front third of the scalp involves about 700–800 grafts, but the procedure will depend on what you want to achieve, and may vary, especially in women.

Dr. Riggs says the technique used in his clinic is the same for men and women. "A lot of times, females thin in the front of the scalp, but if they are diffusely thinning in the front, often they are also diffusely thinning in the donor area," he says. "Then you shouldn't do a transplant because you won't be able to accomplish what the patient wants you to." Dr. Riggs also stresses the importance of determining other possible medical considerations first that might allow for alternative methods of treating loss. "The first thing we do is check out the causes of our patients' hair loss carefully to rule out hormonal imbalances—especially in women. If we find an underlying cause other than **Alopecia**, such as an endocrine issue, the patient may not need a transplant. She should look at other options to correct the underlying problem first. In that case, I would typically refer her to her family doctor or internist for blood work, or have her see an endocrinologist or another specialist. As a matter of fact, if the potential patient is coming from out-of-state, we encourage her to check with other appropriate specialists and do blood work first."

And if Drs. Leavitt and Riggs were at the same table, they might agree on the ideas that revolve around how to address a patient's expectations. "We impress upon the patient that transplantation is not a cure, and that it will simply allow for an improvement in the appearance of thinning or hair loss," says Dr. Riggs. "We try to set the patient's expectations so that they are realistic, and then everyone's happy with results. Our success rate is the same with our female patients as it is with our male patients. And finally, what we do in transplantation is no prediction of what will happen down the road. If the patient continues to lose hair, and many do, and the process has begun in transplantation, the patient will have to decide whether she will accept what happens next or go ahead with further transplanting. For that reason, we keep the grafts small and in that one-, two-, or three-hair range, so that patients will only look like they are thinning if they lose more. The rule we follow is that we plan never to see them again and we handle it that way during surgery, so that whatever the future brings is addressed to the best of our ability in advance."

SCALP REDUCTION

Scalp reductions are different for men. Nine out of ten men who are losing their hair suffer from male pattern baldness, while only one in ten women who are losing their hair suffer from female pattern baldness. Men often have a more clear-cut area to pinpoint for reduction than do most women.

If the area of thinning is too large to cover using transplants from the donor site, the size of the thinning area itself can potentially be made smaller. Among men, it has become more common to have part of the top middle section of the scalp removed to bring the sides closer together so there is a smaller area of the scalp showing. Then hair transplants can be placed in the new, smaller thinned area, ultimately providing the illusion of a nearly full head of hair.

There are some downsides to this procedure, though. More hair may be lost—and lost faster due to the procedure—which will cause some other concerns over time. Scarring may occur and scars may later stretch to wider proportions; there have been reports of skin that has stretched too far, which becomes apparent after healing is complete.

In some cases, doctors are able to expand tissue that has hair before doing a scalp reduction, which reduces the effects of scarring and makes the reduction easier and more aesthetically pleasing. There is also a method of pulling the skin that has hair toward the top or front of the head to help certain women cover their loss. But all of these options were not initially designed with women in mind.

According to the Medical Hair Institute, the procedures involved in scalp reduction and even scalp lifts (see page 232) were first developed after the realization that some of the first transplants looked pretty bad on the men who wore them. Dr. Dominic Brandy, a plastic surgeon who now operates out of Pittsburgh, Pennsylvania, made those initial procedures popular in an effort to provide an alternative to the unsightly transplants of the 1950s that Dr. Leavill described for us earlier. In the past, it helped to minimize the area of loss so you didn't have to see such unnatural-looking grafts. Because today's micrografts and minigrafts look natural, it's not such a necessary procedure.

Reductions can be unsightly. According to the Medical Hair Institute, reduction may provide an instant result, while transplants may take up to a year for the full effect. This may be one reason people opt for reductions. Yet, in a sense, it appears the methods involved in reduction and lifting were never developed as solutions to the actual problem, but as alternative solutions to unpleasant existing solutions.

Where women are concerned, scalp reduction is not a popular solution for hair thinning and loss. Some see it as more drastic, and are afraid of scarring and future loss that will negate some of the results. Most are concerned that they do not know where hair loss will occur next on their scalps, and would rather seek other options for fuller coverage before going to a surgeon for a reduction. Once at the surgeon's office, most women will talk about transplants before they will broach the topic of a scalp reduction. Many find it an extreme option, and choose to examine it last, if at all.

However, there are some situations in which women would be more likely to consider reduction or a scalp lift. Facial cosmetic surgery will alter a woman's hairline sometimes. Female pattern hair loss, at times, may leave acute areas of the scalp free of growing hair. A traumatic incident, such as a car accident or burn, may cause investigation into one of these methods. **Traction Alopecia** might have African-American women in particular interested in these solutions. **Trichotillomania**, a disease in which people pull out their own hair, may provide circumstances that would become less apparent with such procedures, although many would argue that psychological guidance could make a longer-lasting difference.

Still, scalp reduction is not as popular as it once was. "We used to do so many in a week, and now we hardly do that week's worth in a year," says Dr. Leavitt. "We would try to cut the loose skin in an area of baldness and stretch areas with hair to create the overall illusion of more hair. But in doing so, we were making an incision on the head," he continues. "Over time, the incision could become visible as hair continued to be lost. So a wonderful result might look bad later on. Also there were so many variations in healing. So there was a huge upside initially, but over time, results weren't as great as we thought they were. With transplants, we have an advantage over scalp reductions, because we have little or no visible scarring. We can angle or direct each hair individually so that at every stage it looks natural. Our whole philosophy is not to put incisions on the head that may be apparent at any later time."

SCALP LIFTING

The staff at Medical Hair Institute compare the scalp reduction and scalp lift to cars: the reduction would be like a family car, and the lift would be like a turbo racecar. They are similar procedures, they say, but one is more extreme than the other. The Chevy—the reduction—is milder. The Ferrari—the scalp lift—is the extreme version.

In a scalp lift, you are excising part of your scalp as you are in a reduction, but instead of making a ten-sonometer incision, doctors make a thirty-sonometer incision from the front of one ear all the way around to the front of the other. This separates the scalp skin from the scalp all the way underneath the hair under the nape of the neck. In this process, hair-bearing areas are not being stretched out wider and longer; they are being lifted up.

It's rare to find women or men who opt for this solution. Most women experience diffused thinning, unless they have areas in which they have experienced trauma, areas with loss from pulling hair, or other more unusual causes. So loss is more noticeable on the top of the head first, and many women will opt for transplants there since the result will be more positive with potentially less risk.

There are other surgical options, such as suturing false hair into the scalp and expanding hair-bearing areas, but they are not highlighted in this book because they are more controversial and could jeopardize your client's hair health and general health. It's important that you know they exist, but only so you can be wary of them and can discuss all of the options with your clients in an informed manner.

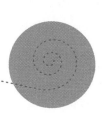

FYI: INTERESTING INFORMATION FOR SERIOUS SURGERY CANDIDATES

According to http://www.howstuffworks.com, a Web site that is a kind of on-line encyclopedia of subjects, there are a few things your clients should know about hair replacement surgery if they are considering it. I have found this list to be helpful, especially to my clients who are new to the subject:

- Hair replacement surgery can be safe when performed by a qualified and experienced surgeon. (It is worthwhile to add sensitive and artistic or creative.)
- Since people are different when it comes to their physical reactions to surgery and healing tendencies, the outcome is never fully predictable, and every surgery contains a risk factor.
- Infection is possible.
- There is the chance that some grafts won't "take" and surgery will have to be repeated—it is not necessarily a one-shot procedure.
- As hair loss progresses after surgery, you can get an unnatural patchy look, especially if new hair is among areas of continued thinning and loss. (The answer, as Dr. Riggs says, is to decide if you will accept this or continue with another procedure.)
- Ask every possible question of your doctor and surgeon. They should be able to answer you in a way that makes you feel comfortable and feel that they know what they are doing.
- Typical surgery sessions take between two and three hours, depending on your needs and what you hope to achieve.
- Ask your doctor to give you an idea of what you might look like after surgery and healing—even though you should keep in mind that it might not be exactly so.
- If you decide to go ahead with surgery, follow all the instructions your surgeon gives you in preparation for the procedure—these might include food and water intake, vitamin consumption, halting of smoking a week or two prior to keep a good level of blood flow to the tissues that will need healing, blood-test work, and hair washing.

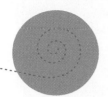

TIPS FOR YOU TO SHARE WITH CLIENTS CONSIDERING SURGERY

The important tip for you to share with any clients who may be considering transplants or any other kind of hair replacement surgery is to go to a specialist specifically and extensively trained in exactly that. Period.

Your client should check with reputable institutions that test these surgeons to find out about the potential surgeon's record. They can try checking with organizations like the American Board of Hair Restoration Surgery, or the International Society of Hair Restoration Surgery, to find out if they have any ratings for a specific doctor, or even if they have received formal complaints about him or her. They should do their homework, and then find references. It's important to know as much as possible about this person, the same way a person would for a surgeon of any other nature who would be cutting them open.

Your client should see if she can meet someone who is a walking example of the doctor's work, talk with that person about exactly what was done, and perhaps ask if she can closely examine the person's scalp. Her aim is to see if that person is a satisfied female patient.

TURN-KEY BUSINESS DEVELOPMENT

CHAPTER
6

Congratulations. You've come a long way in a short time. Let's review what you have learned:

- You know the five key ingredients of healthy, beautiful hair.
- You've learned about the causes of women's hair thinning and hair loss, and you've seen the drastic consequences that hair loss can have on a woman's self-esteem and self-image.
- You've learned how to conduct a detailed consultation and make an accurate assessment of your client's situation, and you know how to recommend the best alternatives for each client.
- You've familiarized yourself with the range of hair-restoration and hair-replacement solutions, from extensions and integrations to duplications and complete cranial prostheses.
- You know the design elements to consider and processes to follow in creating each solution, and you know how to select and use the best materials.
- You know when to recommend, and where to find, the best tools, products, treatments, and therapies to support and nourish your clients' growing hair and to enable them to maintain their hair-replacement systems.

You've had a good look at what hair restoration is about. You've seen what's involved—for the client and for the practitioner. You've been guided step-by-step through the hands-on aspects of the work. You're already far better informed about hair restoration and hair replacement than most professionals in the hair-care and beauty industries.

Now that you're fully acquainted with what goes into a top notch hair-restoration practice, it's time to decide whether a career in hair restoration is right for you.

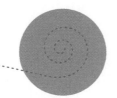

IS HAIR RESTORATION THE RIGHT BUSINESS FOR YOU?

To find out whether establishing a hair-restoration business is the right step for you, consider the following questions seriously, and pay attention to your answers.

1. What are your career objectives?

2. Is financial gain important to you? Are there other aspects of your work that are equally important? More important? How would you rate your priorities?

3. How much of your time, energy, and self are you willing to invest in your work?

4. Do you want to work in someone else's salon? Own your own business? Be a solo practitioner? Employ other people? Partner with a salon as a specialty department?

5. What do you like most about the hair-care business? The salon/spa business? What do you like least?

6. Do you think of yourself as a hair cutter? A stylist? A designer? A beauty consultant?

7. Do you look on your work as a job? A career? A vocation? An art? A ministry?

8. Is your work creatively fulfilling? Is that important to you?

9. Why are you thinking of specializing in hair replacement? Is hair replacement an area of personal interest for you? Does hair replacement attract you primarily for commercial reasons?

10. Do you consider hair replacement a service that is vital and necessary for your clients? Or do you see it as a mere option, with limited appeal?

11. What would you say is your foremost motivation for mastering hair replacement skills? Are you looking for a creative challenge? Do you have a strong urge to help and support others? Is your primary incentive financial gain?

12. Can you see yourself specializing in work that:

- gives you personal fulfillment and creative satisfaction?

- provides a transformational service to those in need?

- offers opportunity for financial reward by addressing the demands of an exploding market?

Turn-key Business Development

In case you didn't notice, number 12 was a leading question.

I believe that you can have it all. You can do work that you're passionate about. You can touch people's lives. You can hold up a different mirror for people who are struggling, and help them find new encouragement and hope. And you can reap financial gain by capitalizing on the needs of a demographic group that can only grow.

The question is: Is that what you want? If your answer is yes, then you're ready to look at the nuts-and-bolts of running a hair-replacement business.

BUSINESS STRUCTURE AND DEVELOPMENT

You know which category you're starting out in: solo practitioner, operator in an established salon/spa, or employer of others in your own business. You've decided on whether you want to make hair replacement your full-time profession or a component of an established full-service business. Certain considerations will change, or course, depending on those choices. You can adapt the information provided below to your own specific circumstances.

There are four key components to consider in developing a hair-restoration business, once you have decided to concentrate on this market.

1. Target-market assessment and financial projection

2. Physical layout and equipment

3. Manufacturer and product-line relationships

4. Marketing plan

After you review these components in detail, you will be able to decide which level of investment best suits your current circumstances and long-range goals.

1a. Target-market assessment

To assess your potential target market, you need to break it down into two categories: your current salon population, and your community population.

- Current salon population

  Out of the women's segment of your current customer base, you can estimate that one out of four will need some form of hair restoration. Assume that 20 percent will make a decision within 12 months of your adding hair-restoration services to your salon/spa.

- Community population

  Again, out of the total population of women in your community above the age of 29, one out of four will have a demonstrable need for some form of hair restoration. Of these, you can assume that two percent will elect to obtain these services from your salon.

1b. Target-market financial projection

In estimating your target-market potential, you should use a conservative average purchase of $500 for a single hair restoration.

The average expenses:

- Cost of goods and materials: 30 percent
- Sales commission: 10 percent

Turn-key Business Development

- Service commission: 20 percent

- Gross profit margin: remaining 40 percent

Here's the math:

Hair-restoration sale (100 percent):	$500
Cost of goods and supplies (30 percent):	−150
	$350
Sales commission (10 percent):	−50
	$300
Service commission (20 percent):	−100
Gross profit margin (40 percent):	$200

Two things you should be aware of:

- The above figures do not include income from the on-going services of hair-restoration and specialty-products retail sales — these represent additional income.

- Average replacement time for a hair-restoration system is about 9–18 months; this represents additional income that you would add to a 24-month projection.

2. Physical layout and equipment

Investment start-up costs will depend on what you want to focus on (the type of hair-replacement program you will offer in your salon/spa) and the level of décor you select. You have four escalating options; the one you choose will depend on the type of equipment and facility you select.

Level 1

Behind the chair, in any space you select in the salon.

A rollabout cart, with the appropriate equipment, can be used at any existing station. This level is ideal, if you want to concentrate on the hair-extension market.

Investment range: $1,000–$5,000

Level 2

Enhancement of unused space within your salon/spa.

The rollabout cart can be added to underused space, such as a facial or massage room in your salon; this enables you to offer a measure of privacy to your clients, as circumstances permit. While this approach may limit your ability to implement a full range of services for your clients (see Level 3 below), in the initial stages of your hair-restoration practice, it will allow you flexibility and the opportunity to expand as business growth permits.

Investment range: $5,000–$15,000

Level 3

A dedicated space within your salon/spa.

With this option, you can dedicate a specific room to hair restoration and extensions. This approach allows you to provide services in complete privacy to clients in need of all types of hair restoration. Combining all the components of consultation, design, provision of service, and client training in hair-system maintenance, Level 3 enables you to maintain a complete, freestanding operation within your salon/spa. In a dedicated space, you can also set up a permanent display of retail products and accessories, such as turbans, hair additions, specialty accessories, and maintenance products. (See description of the layout of an ideal hair-restoration suite below.)

Investment range: $15,000–$35,000

Level 4

Complete hair-restoration salon/spa. This is a stand-alone business operation dedicated exclusively to clients seeking hair-restoration solutions in a setting that guarantees privacy and a full range of specialty services. This approach follows the medical spa collaboration model that the medical community and salon/spa operators are now offering.

Investment range: $25,000 and up

The illustrated model on page 245 will show you how you can take a dedicated space ranging in size from 8' by 8' to a 12' by 12' room and turn it into a total-approach hair-restoration suite that will completely facilitate all the components for an efficient and profitable operation.

Component 1—Consultation Station   Stores the TV/VCR combination on a specially designed hydraulic shelf, which is used during the consultation to show the client her customized options and educate her about what solutions best fit her individual needs. When not in use, the TV disappears into the cabinet, which once again becomes counter space.

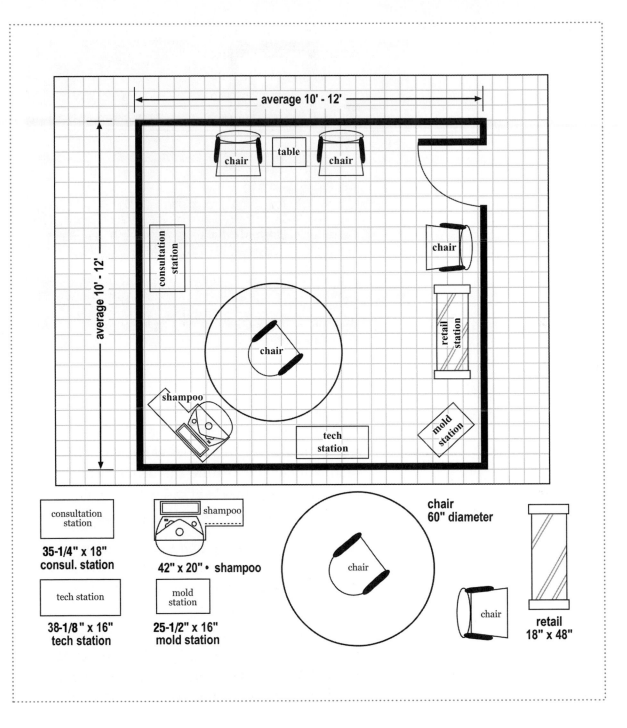

average 10' - 12'

average 10' - 12'

chair

table

chair

consultation station

chair

retail station

chair

shampoo

mold station

tech station

consultation station

35-1/4" x 18" consul. station

tech station

38-1/8" x 16" tech station

shampoo

42" x 20" • shampoo

mold station

25-1/2" x 16" mold station

chair
60" diameter

chair

chair

chair

retail
18" x 48"

Turn-key Business Development

A unique presentation of mannequin heads is also stored in this first station, along with hair samples and color rings with swatches of hair color. The half-head mannequins feature the actual product in a cut-away view, so the client can see the quality of the materials and the customized hand-made designs.

Component 2—Molding and Design Station Holds the tools and forms that are needed to fit the client. The state-of-the-art molding and casting component used by the hair-replacement specialist provides a precise measurement of the shape and dimension of the skull and the head, thereby eliminating the guesswork involved in creating a custom hair system.

The station also includes drawers for storing hair samples, density charts, and design order forms.

Component 3—Wet Station   At this location, a client's hair is washed, reconditioned, and repaired prior to the application of the hair system. A custom-designed counter top covers the shampoo bowl when it is not in use and provides additional counter space.

Component 4—Technical Station   Employs a specially designed hydraulic shelf fitted with a tripod and mannequin head, which facilitates the fitting and application of hair systems ranging from extensions to total coverage hairpieces. To complete the operation,

tape, adhesives, and technical and styling tools are all within arm's reach of this station.

Component 5—Retail Station   The retail area. This is where a client is instructed in the care of the hair system, and is introduced to the range of products and services that will help maintain it in optimal condition. (Shown with wet station)

The room design and build-out take approximately one month and cost $8,000–$15,000. The rooms are cus-

tomized to complement any salon's décor. The rooms can be finished with framed "before" and "after" photographs of clients that include their personal stories and chosen methods of hair restoration (e.g., extensions, duplication, integration, or full-cranial prosthesis or artwork to set the mood of choice).

3. *Manufacturer and product-line relationships*   In the resource section of this book, you will find a list of manufacturers specializing in hair-restoration products and services of proven quality, as well as educational institutes that can support your training needs.

Naturally, the quality of your hair-replacement systems will greatly depend on the quality of the materials you use to create and maintain them, and the smooth running of your business will depend on the relationships you develop with your providers. As you begin to build your hair-replacement practice, you'll also be sampling products and services to see which manufacturers deliver the best quality materials and the most reliable service.

While the list offered in this book is not comprehensive—the hair-replacement field is growing every day—each company named has demonstrated over time the quality of its products and the integrity of its business practices. These companies will work with you to support your development as a top-notch hair-restoration specialist.

4. *Marketing Plan*   The successful hair-restoration practice employs an integration of promotional strategies designed to develop and expand community awareness of:

- the pervasive need for hair restoration (one out of every four women!)

- the availability of local hair-restoration services

a. Marketing in the salon/spa

One out of every four women who walks into a salon or spa needs hair restoration. The other three have a friend or family member who needs it. Salon staff should be trained to recognize which clients should be told about hair restoration and to promote the on-staff hair-restoration specialist. In addition, the salon should prominently display a poster and/or information center (offering brochures, fact sheets, etc.) with key facts about hair-loss problems and hair-replacement solutions.

The time to start your in-house marketing is while you're building your hair-replacement suite in your salon/spa. Plan an open house to introduce the new methods, equipment, and services to your existing clients and the local community. Send invitations to clients and potential clients, send press releases to the local media, and contact key individuals and medical practices in the local community.

Don't overlook the extremely effective technique of using testimonials and before-and-after photos of your current clients in all your literature (posters, brochures, print ads, press releases, open-house invitations, etc.), and plan to use your most successful clients as models at the open house.

b. Marketing in the community

Marketing within the community ranges from getting posters up in suitable locations and making use of the traditional advertising and promotional approaches (newspapers, radio, television) to hosting educational forums for clients and the public, and sending ambassador programs to hospitals and private practices.

c. Direct mail

In addition to marketing approaches targeted to groups or the community at large, postcards introducing your new products and services and announcing the date of your open house can be sent to individual households and potential referral sources (e.g., medical practices).

d. Referral development

Outreach initiatives (such as the ambassador programs) to medical associations, health organizations, hospitals, and physicians will ensure that you and your services are known in your community. The American Cancer Society, for example, is an excellent referral source. Your local chapter needs to know that your salon/spa offers hair-restoration services.

e. Charity involvement—giving back

Wigs for Kids, incorporated in 1983, is a nonprofit organization in Rocky River, Ohio, that my wife, Zina, and I founded. It provides custom-made hair systems, at no charge, to children who have lost their hair from medical causes, and whose families cannot afford to buy a hairpiece. Through the years, Wigs for Kids has given away thousands of hair systems to needy children. No child has ever been turned away.

Wigs for Kids is both a wonderful charity and a superb marketing tool. Women and girls—and many longhaired men!—have cut their ponytails and donated them to Wigs for Kids. Businesses and community groups throughout the country hold fundraisers for Wigs for Kids. Salons run specials for customers donating their ponytails to Wigs for Kids. Individuals—adults and children—have made Wigs for Kids their special cause, and waged successful campaigns for contributions from their friends, families, colleagues, and communities.

The media love to cover these stories. Becoming a designated Wigs for Kids affiliate creates

Proud Sponsor of

WIGS FOR KIDS®

automatic opportunities to publicize a hair-replacement practice or salon/spa year-round—and it's all for a worthy cause.

For details on how you and your salon/spa can get involved, visit http://www.wigsforkids.org or e-mail info@wigsforkids.org.

FINAL WORD
FROM THE AUTHOR

As hairdressers, when we turn our clients toward the mirror to show them finished styles, the reward of satisfied customers speaks for itself. But when you have finished restoring lost hair to a woman and turn her into the mirror, in addition to her outward beauty, you have also restored her inner beauty, and that is priceless. Outer beauty is a visual thing, but inner beauty is unseen and much more difficult to care for.

Beauty begins within,

Jeffrey Paul

GLOSSARY

ALOPECIA Medical term for baldness.

ALOPECIA AREATA Medical term for patchy hair loss on the scalp. Alopecia areata is believed to be caused by a disorder of the immune system.

ALOPECIA TOTALIS A form of alopecia areata in which hair is lost from the entire scalp.

ALOPECIA UNIVERSALIS A form of alopecia areata in which hair is lost on the entire body.

ANAGEN The growing phase of the hair cycle.

ANAGEN EFFLUVIUM Hair loss caused by chemotherapeutic drugs.

ANDROGENETIC ALOPECIA Hair loss resulting from a genetic predisposition to effects of DHT on the hair follicles. Also termed female pattern baldness and male pattern baldness.

BLOCK A head-shaped form usually made of canvas-covered cork or Styrofoam, to which the hair system is secured for fitting, cleaning, color, and styling.

BONDING A method of attaching hair extensions in which hair wefts or single strands are attached with an adhesive or a glue gun.

CATAGEN The transitional phase of the hair cycle occurring after anagen and before telogen.

CORTEX The main structural part of the hair fiber.

CUSTOM Refers to a product designed by you for your specific needs.

CUTICLE The outermost portion of the hair fiber.

DAILY-WEAR CLIENT Take on and off daily by the use of tapes or clips.

DENSITY Refers to the number of hairs inserted in the system, for example, light density, medium density, heavy density.

DERMAL PAPILLA A structure at the base of the hair follicle, rich in blood vessels that supply nutrients to construct keratin.

DIHYDROTESTOSTERONE (DHT) A hormone formed when the enzyme 5 alpha-reductase interacts with testosterone; is believed to destroy hair follicles in adrogenetic alopecia.

DONOR SITE An area of skin with healthy hair follicles that is surgically transplanted onto bald patches.

EXFOLIATING SCRUB (FOLLI-SCRUB) Used on scalp to remove dead skin cells before full-head bonding.

EXTENDED-WEAR One of the most popular methods of wearing hair by using medical grade adhesives, or by sewing on. Stays in place two to six weeks; also called permanent attachment.

FOLLICLE A sack-like structure just below the surface of the scalp; hair grows from the follicle.

GRAFTING A variety of procedures for moving hair-bearing scalp from the back of the head to a recipient site. The most widely used types of grafting are slit grafts, micro-grafting, and mini-grafting.

GRAFTS Transplanted hair.

HACKLE AND DRAWING CARD The hackle is used to blend hair colors for ventilating. The drawing card is used to hold hair after blending and helps keep hair straight and untangled.

HAIR EXTENSIONS Hair additions that are secured to the base of the natural hair in order to add length, volume, texture, or color.

HAIRPIECE A small wig used to cover the top or crown of the head; add-on hair that is integrated with the client's own hair; toupee.

HAND-TIED OR HAND-KNOTTED WIG A wig made by inserting individual strands of hair into mesh foundations and knotting them with a needle.

INTEGRATION HAIRPIECE A hairpiece with an opening in the base through which the client's own hair is pulled to blend with the hair (natural or synthetic) of the hairpiece.

KERATIN A tough but elastic protein from which hair is constructed.

KNOTS Hair circled around and through the base material and tied to itself at the root area.

LACE FRONT An extension of nylon netting or silk gauze that hair is ventilated into, leaving approximately one-eighth to one-quarter inch extension of lace without hair to be glued to skin with adhesive, then becoming undetectable.

LOOPED KNOT Hair inserted into the base and brought back up through the base in a loop, but not knotted. Can be used only on PU bases or tape tabs.

MACHINE-MADE WIGS Wigs made by machine, not by hand, by feeding wefts through a sewing machine, then sewing them together to form the base and shape of the wigs.

MEDULLA The innermost portion of the hair fiber.

MICRO-GRAFT A grouping of one to three hairs used in a hair transplant and inserted into needle holes.

MICRO-LINKS Hair is pulled through and the link is squeezed shut to hold the hair tight. Smaller than tube links. Can be sewn to a base.

MINIATURIZATION The destructive process by which DHT shrinks hair follicles and causes them to deteriorate over time, thus triggering hair loss.

MINI-GRAFT Small rectangles or circles of three to eight follicles each.

MINOXIDIL The generic name for the drug Rogaine and other products approved for treating hair loss in men and women. Minoxidil is available as an over-the-counter drug in a two percent solution as well as a prescription drug in a five percent concentration.

NON-SCARRING ALOPECIA A broad category of different types of hair loss, including androgenetic alopecia. In non-scarring alopecia, the hair follicle remains intact, thus increasing the likelihood that hair loss can be reversed.

NONVELLUS HAIR Hairs that are thick and dark. Normal scalp hair is considered nonvellus hair. Also called terminal hair.

PERIMETER Refers to the outer edge or border of the system. Can be finished in several ways, depending on the attachment method.

PLASTER MOLD OR FIBERGLASS MOLD Plaster pares gauze strips or fiberglass gauze strips that will form to the head to make a positive mold.

POLYURETHANE Used as a border to create a better form; comes in three different thicknesses: light, medium, and heavy.

RECESSION Refers to the shape of the front.

REMY HUMAN HAIR Refers to hair that has been re-toned with textile dyes; has nearly all the cuticle left.

ROOT TURNED HAIR Hair processed with the cuticle all in one direction.

SCALLOPS An irregular front hairline created by one of our six standard scallops. Used on polyurethane in front. Not recommended with under-venting or baby hair.

SCALP REDUCTION A procedure that involves the surgical removal of a strip of hairless scalp to reduce the total area of baldness.

SECTIONS OF THE HEAD These are the six sections of the hair system.

SEMI-HAND-TIED WIGS Wigs constructed with a combination of synthetic hair and hand-tied human hair.

SINGLE HAIR IMPLANT Refers to the number of strands of hair which are ventilated into one knot. Single hair implant refers to one or two hairs per knot. Cannot be done on heavy density systems.

SKIN PREP Seals the scalp eliminating oil secretions; used only where there is tape, not in the bonding track area under the adhesive. This product will help extend the time tape will hold.

TAPE TEMPLATE Use of saran film over head and clear scotch tape overlaid to form a positive template pattern.

TELOGEN The resting phase of the hair cycle.

TELOGEN EFFLUVIUM The second most common form of hair loss; usually the result of severe stress, illness, major surgery, childbirth, and the use of certain medications. It can be delayed (occurring a few months after the stressful incident) or chronic (unresolved).

TESTOSTERONE A male hormone that promotes the development of male characteristics.

TOUPELON A synthetic fiber used in blending to develop an ash base color.

TRACTION ALOPECIA Hair loss caused by tightly pulled hair styles.

TRICHOTILLOMANIA Habitual hair-pulling.

TURNED HAIR Wig hair in which the root end of every hair strand is sewn into the base so that the cuticles of all hair strands slope in the same direction.

UNDER-VENT A row of hair vented into bottom of base along the outside perimeter. Can also be used in the front to help conceal the front edge; not recommended for lace or scallop fronts.

VELLUS The soft, fluffy post-natal hair that remains on the entire body, except for the palms of the hands, soles of the feet, and other normally hairless areas.

VENTILATING The process of knotting hair into a system by the use of a small hooked needle.

WEFTS Strips of human or artificial hair woven by hand or machine onto a thread.

WIG Artificial covering for the head consisting of a network of interwoven hair.

YAK HAIR Hair found on the under belly of the yak; can be used in place of synthetic for gray hair.

RESOURCES

Despite the reluctance of the general public to open up to the subject of women's hair loss, there are a wide variety of trustworthy experts and sources of information available to help you and your clients along, no matter what stage of thinning or loss they are experiencing. And since the World Wide Web burst onto the scene, there's a new source of information for you to explore.

"Well," you may be thinking, "I've already read this book. What more do I need to know?" If that's what you're thinking, then many thanks! I hope that after reading this, you will find that you have significant understanding of all facets of hair loss and what you can do to address it. But I want you to know about the resources available to you—at least the ones I have found to be helpful and responsible—in the event that you need to look further and understand more about the subject in general or one of the solutions described in this book. Perhaps you will want to know more about the medical side of things, the psychological element of the problem, or the suppliers and specialists that are well-known in the industry. In the event that you do, this section provides recommended resources to help you along.

It includes all of the experts cited in this book and where they can be found. It also contains other sources of information and services that are well respected but not included in the previous chapters. These resources are grouped into categories for ease of use.

Hair Restoration Business Consultants

Jeffrey Paul Restoring Beautiful Hair Institute
21330 Center Ridge Road
Rocky River, Ohio 44116
(440) 333-8939
http://www.beautifulhairagain.com
also the Hair Replacement and Cosmetic Reconstruction
Institute (HRCR)
(800) 883-7667

Organizations and Associations

Alopecia Help and Advice, Ltd.
33 Burbank Road
Grangemouth, United Kingdom FK3 8RU
http://www.alopeciascotland.co.uk

American Academy of Dermatology (AAD)
930 East Woodfield Rd.
Schaumburg, IL 60173
(847) 330-0230
http://www.aad.org

American Board of Hair Restoration Surgery
185–25 Torrence Avenue
Lansing, IL 60438
(708) 474-2600
http://www.abhrs.org

American Board of Nutrition
University of Alabama at Birmingham
Department of Nutrition Sciences
1675 University Boulevard/WEBB 232
Birmingham, Alabama 35294
(205) 975-8788
http://www.uab.edu/nusc/abn.htm

American College of Surgeons (ACS)
633 North Saint Clair Street
Chicago, IL 60611-3211
(312) 202-5000
http://www.facs.org

American Dietetic Association
216 West Jackson Blvd.
Chicago, IL 60606
(312) 899-0040 or (800) 877-1600
http://www.adaf.org

American Hair Loss Council
125 Seventh Street
Suite 625
Pittsburgh, PA 15222
(412)765-3666
903-561-1107 Texas
312-321-5128 Illinois
800-274-8717 consumer hotline
888-873-9719 toll free
http://www.ahlc.org

American Medical Association (AMA)
515 North State St.
Chicago, IL 60610
(312) 464-5000
http://www.ama-assn.org

American Medical Women's Association (AMWA)
801 N. Fairfax St.
Suite 400
Alexandria, VA 22314
(703) 838-0500
http://www.amwa-doc.org

American Pharmaceutical Association (APhA)
2215 Constitution Avenue, NW
Washington, DC 20037
(202) 628-4410 or (800) 237-2742
http://www.aphanet.org

American Psychiatric Association (APA)
1400 K Street, NW
Washington, DC 20005
(888) 357-7924
http://www.psych.org

American Society of Hair Restoration Surgery
(a division of the American Academy of Cosmetic Surgery)
737 North Michigan Avenue
Suite 820
Chicago, IL 60611
312-981-6760
http://www.cosmeticsurgery.org

Resources

Cancer Research Institute
681 Fifth Avenue
New York, NY 10022-4209
(212) 688-7515 or (800) 99-CANCER
http://www.cancerresearch.org

Children With Hairloss Foundation
22215 Heron River Drive
Rockland, MI 48173
(734) 379-7048 or (866) 424-7567
http://www.childrenwithhairloss.org

Federation of State Medical Boards
Federation Place
400 Fuller Wiser Road
Suite 300
Euless, TX 76039-3855
(817) 868-4000
http://www.fsmb.org

International Association of Trichologists
185 Elizabeth Street
Suite 919
Sydney, Australia NSW 2000
Tel. (011) (02) 9267-1384
http://www.trichology.edu.au

International Food Information Council
IFIC Foundation
1100 Connecticut Avenue NW
Suite 430
Washington D.C. 20036

(202) 296-6540
http://www.ific.org

International Society of Hair Restoration Surgery (ISHRS)
13 South Second Street
Geneva, IL 60134
(630) 262-5399 or (800) 444-2737
http://www.ishrs.org

National Alopecia Areata Foundation
710 C Street
Suite 11
PO Box 150760
San Rafael, CA 94915
415-456-4644 or (617) 239-3333
http://www.alopeciaareata.com or www.naaf.org

National Psoriasis Foundation
6600 SW 92nd Street
Suite 300
Portland OR 97223
(503) 244-7404 or (800) 723-9166
http://www.psoriasis.org

National Women's Health Information Center—HHS
8550 Arlington Blvd.
Suite 300
Fairfax, Virginia 22031
(800) 994-WOMAN (96626)
http://www.4woman.org

Resources

Pharmaceutical Research and Manufacturers of America
1100 Fifteenth Street, NW
Washington, DC 20005
(202) 835-3400
http://www.phrma.org

The Salon Association
15825 North 71st St.
Suite 100
Scottsdale, AZ 85254
(800)-211-4TSA
http://www.thesalonassociation.com

Society for Women's Health Research
1828 L Street, NW
Suite 625
Washington, DC 20036
(202) 223-8224
http://www.womens-health.org

The Wellness Community (free support in dealing with disease
and medical issues)
2716 Ocean Park Blvd.
Suite 1040
Santa Monica, CA 90405
(310) 314-2555
http://www.wellness-community.org

Wigs For Kids
(440) 333-4433
info@wigsforkids.org
http://www.wigsforkids.org

The Women's Institute for Fine and Thinning Hair
Sponsored by Rogaine
Pharmacia Consumer Health Care
PO Box 90541
Allentown, PA 18109
(877) 554-HAIR
http://www.womenshairinstitute.com

Hair Restoration Specialists

Feeling's Women's Health
285 Sills Road, Building 2, Suite A
East Patchoge, NY 11772
(631) 475-0400
Miriam Jung

G.P. Custom Hair Inc.
1078 Tunnel Road
Asheville, NC 28805
(628) 296-6371
Grady Parham

Gilberto Hair Center
911 N.W. 27th Avenue
Miami, FL 33125
(305) 461-0077
Gilberto Fabies

Hair Club For Men and Women
1515 South Federal Highway
Suite 401
Boca Raton, FL 33432

(888) 888-8986 or (800) HAIR-CLUB (424-7258)
http://www.hairclub.com

Hair Extension Technologies
7853 Gunn Highway, PMB 253
Tampa, FL 33626
(313) 625-7843
Bobbi Russell

Hair Response
3385 North Arlington Heights Road, Suite J
Arlington Heights, IL 60004
(547) 870-9799
Amy Goldberg

Jeffrey Paul Restoring Beautiful Hair Center
21330 Center Ridge Road
Rocky River, Ohio 44116
(440) 333-8939
http://www.beautifulhairagain.com
also the Hair Replacement and Cosmetic Reconstruction
Institute (HRCR)
(800) 883–7667
and Wigs For Kids
(440) 333-4433
http://www.wigsforkids.org

Robin Knight
2541 Steeple Chase Drive
Miamisburg, OH 45342
(937) 389-4196
Robin Knight

Salon 41 Inc.
4280 Cleveland Avenue, Suite D
Fort Meyers, FL 33901
(239) 418-1312
Vernon Smith

Young Hair Inc.
1928 East High Street
Springfield, OH 45505
(937) 324-4301
Patty Young

Cosmetic Therapists and Color Analysis

Color Me Beautiful
14900 Conference Center Drive
Chantilly, VA 20151
(800) COLOR-ME (265-6763)
http://www.colormebeautiful.com

Marianne Zarlinga
Cosmetic Therapist
Skin Secrets
8527 Ridge Road
North Royalton, Ohio 44133
(440) 582-8550

Doctors and Scientists

Dr. Alan Bauman
Bauman Medical Group, P.A.
6861 SW 18th Street
Suite 102
Boca Raton , FL 33428
(561) 394-0024
http://www.baumanmedical.com

Dr. Wilma Bergfeld
Head of Dermatopathology, Dermatology and
Clinical Research in Dermatology
The Cleveland Clinic Foundation
(also the first woman President of the American
Academy of Dermatology)
9500 Euclid Avenue
Cleveland, OH 44195
(216) 444-5722 or (800) 223-2273, ext. 48950
http://www.clevelandclinic.org

Dr. Larry Lee Bosley
Bosley Medical Group
9100 Wilshire Boulevard—East Tower
Beverly Hills, California 90212
(800) 352-2244
http://www.bosley.com

Dr. Dominic Brandy
Enhanced Images Cosmetic Surgery
2275 Swallow Hill Road—Building 2400
Pittsburgh, PA 15220
(412) 429-1151

Dr. Rebecca Caserio
Fox Chapel Dermatology
241 Freeport Rd
Suite 7
Aspinwall, PA 15215
(412) 784-1606
http://www.foxchapelderm.com

Dr. Angela Christiano
Associate Professor of Genetics and Development,
Dept. of Dermatology
Hair Research & Treatment Center
Columbia University College of Physicians & Surgeons
(212) 305-9565;
or the Research & Treatment Center
(212) 305-5317
http://www.columbia.edu or
http://cpmcnet.columbia.edu/dept/derm/hairloss/index.html

Dr. Zoe Draelos
2444 North Main Street
High Point, NC 27262
(336) 841-2040
zdraelos@northstate.net

Dr. Gary S. Hitzig
44 East 67th St.
Suite 1A
New York, NY 10021
(212) 744-4668 or (800) HAIR-USA

Resources

Dr. Matt Leavitt
Medical Hair Restoration
120 International Parkway
Suite 240
Heathrow, FL 32746
(888) 238-3376
http://www.medicalhairrestoration.com

Dr. Amy McMichael
Wake Forest University Baptist Medical Center
Department of Dermatology
Medical Center Boulevard
Winston-Salem, NC 27157
(336) 716-3926
http://www.wfubmc.edu

Dr. Paradi Mirmirani
University Hospitals of Cleveland
Dermatology Department
UHHS Chagrin Highlands Medical Center
3909 Orange Place
Orange Village, OH 44122
(216) 360-8808
http://www.uhhs.com

Dr. Vera H. Price
Director, UCSF Hair Research Center
Department of Dermatology
Box 0363–350 Parnassus Street—404
UC San Francisco
San Francisco, CA 94143
(415) 476-3636

Dr. Geoffrey Redmond
The Hormone Help Center
133 East 73rd Street
New York, NY 10021
(212) 861-9000
http://www.hormonehelpny.com

Dr. Paul Riggs
Coastal Medical Group (cold laser transplantation)
13923 Icot Blvd.
Building 8—Suite 807
Clearwater, FL 33760
(727) 535-8009
http://www.hair-transplants.com

Dr. Gary Ross
500 Sutter
San Francisco, CA
(415) 398-0555

Dr. Ronald Savin
Clinical Professor of Dermatology at Yale University
President, Savin Center, P.C.
134 Park Street
New Haven, CT 06511
203-865-6143
http://www.savincenter.com

Dr. Susan Craig Scott
6 East 78th Street
New York, NY 10021
(212) 288-9922

Manufacturers and Suppliers

Brilliant Products
7000 Fleury Way
Pittsburgh, PA 15208
Tel. (800) 522-4512
Fax (412) 361-2844

Chrissy V. Extension Systems
18565 Soledad Cyn. Rd
Suite 132pmb
Santa Clarita, CA 91351
(661) 373-HAIR (4247)
http://www.chrissyv.com

Custom Formulations Inc.
507 Conrad/P.O. Box 200
Cologne, MN 55322
Tel. (800) 328-5906
Fax (952) 466-5640

DermMatch Topical Shading
PO Box 878
Venice, FL 34284
(941) 408-9225 or (800) 826-2824
http://www.dermmatch.com

Garland Drake International (supplier of natural human hair)
3900 Birch Street #105
Newport Beach, CA 92660
(714) 250-2965 or (800) 426-9197
http://www.garlanddrake.com

Great American Coverup
From More Hair Cosmetics, NY
1-800-874-HAIR

Great Lengths
Eva Gabor International
5775 Deramus Avenue
Kansas City, Missouri 64120
(816) 231-3700
http://www.greatlengths.com

Hair Additions
21330 Center Ridge Road
Rocky River, Ohio 44116
(800)883-7667
http://www.hairadditions.com

Hair & Compounds, Inc.
7820 Burnet Avenue
Unit A
Van Nuys, CA 91405
(818) 997-8810
http://www.haircompounds.com

HairMax
2650 N. Military Trail
Suite 360
Boca Raton, FL 33431
Telephone: 561-417-0200
Fax: 561-892-0747
Toll Free: 866-527-3726
(866) LASERCOMB (527–3726)
http://www.hairmax.com

Hair Support
18684 Lake Drive East
Chanhassen, MN 55317
(800) 328-0311 or (800) 535-5980
http://www.hairsupport.com

Harmonix Corporation
Plum Park Center
141 NW 20th Street
Suite H1
Boca Raton, FL 33431
(888) 446-3747
http://www.harmonixcorp.com

International Hair Goods, Inc.
(800) 328-6182
http://www.internationalhairgoods.com

Invisible Hair
1946 Monte Vista Drive
Vista, California 92084
1-800-300-8487
http://www.invisiblehair.com

Isa Designs
4419 Church Hill Blvd.
University Heights, Ohio 44118
(216) 381-1837
http://www.isadesigns.com

Just In Time
PO Box 27693
Philadelphia, PA 19118
(215) 247-8777
http://www.softhats.com

Kevis Rejuvenation Programs, Inc.
246 Robertson Blvd.
Beverly Hills, CA 90211
(888) 635-HAIR (4247)
http://www.kevis.com

Laser Hair Care
c/o Laser Science AB
Box 22 09, S-103-15
Stockholm, Sweden
http://www.laser-sci.se

Look of Love
555A North Michigan Ave.
Kenilworth, NJ 07033
(800) 526-7627
http://www.lookoflove.com

Marie-Josée
52 State Street
Montpelier, VT 05602
(866) R22-HAIR (722-4247)
http://www.mariejosee.com

Mega Hair International
(800) 233-MEGA (6342)
http://www.megahair.com

Micro Point Link/Cyberhair (see also International Hair Goods,
Hair Support)
http://www.micropointlink.com

Nanogen (shake on fibers and stay spray)
Tel. 011-44-020-8349-2000

New Concepts Hair Goods, Inc.
1450 SW 3rd St.
Suite A-9
Pompano Beach, FL 33069
(954) 545-9722 or (800) 676-6244
http://www.newconceptshair.com

New Hair Technology, Inc. (vacuum prosthetics)
65 West 55th Street
Suite 4B
New York, NY 10019
(212) 581-5900 or (800) 434-4552
http://www.nuhair.com

Nioxin
1781 Westfork Drive
Lithia Springs, GA 30122
(800) 628-9890
http://www.nioxin.com

Nisim International
204 Wilkinson Road
Brampton, Ontario, Canada L6T 4M4
(905) 451-7772 or 1-800-65-NISIM (64746)
http://www.nisim.com

NuGen HP
c/o Star Health and Beauty
1033 Franklin Road
Suite 9-172
Marietta, GA 30067
(888) 246-8670
http://www.nugenhp.com

On-Rite Company
5130 North State Road 7
Ft. Lauderdale, FL 33319
(800) 982-3834

Paul Mitchell
(800) THE-SALON (843-7256)
http://www.paulmitchell.com
(no information on hair loss on the site itself)

Phytologie
c/o Ales Group USA, Inc.
625 Madison Avenue
New York, NY 10022
(800) 648-0349

Pivot Point (educators for salons)
1791 West Howard Street
Chicago, IL 60626
(312) 973-0500, (800) 886-4247 or (800) 621-1501
http://www.pivot-point.com

René of Paris
(818) 908-3100
http://www.reneofparis.com

Revivogen Advanced Skin and Hair, Inc.
9911 West Pico Blvd.
Suite 808
Los Angeles, CA 90035
(888) 616-HAIR (4247) or (909) 873-3597
http://www.revivogen.com

Rogaine For Women
Pharmacia Corporation
100 Route 206 North
Peapack, NJ 07977
(908) 901-8000 or (888) 768-5501
about Rogaine for Women: (800) 764-2463
http://www.rogaineforwomen.com

Solano International
8044 Lawndale
Skokie, IL 60076
(847) 675-0087

Spencer Forrest, Inc.
64 Post Road West
Westport, Connecticut 06880
(203) 454-2733 or (800) 416-3325
http://www.regrow.com

Tricomin (follicle therapy spray, shampoo line)
ProCyte Corporation
P.O. Box 808
Redmond, WA 98073
(425) 869-1239
http://www.tricomin.com or http://www.procyte.com

Trigenesis (topical and capsules)
(800) 678-7860
Ecoly International
9232 Eton Avenue
Chatsworth, CA 91311
(818) 718-6982 or (800) 848-3383
http://www.ecoly.com

Veeco Manufacturing
1217 West Washington Blvd.
Chicago, IL 60607
Tel. (800) 635-3772
Fax (312) 666-7945
www.veeco-mfg.com

Viviscal

  US West—Natural Hair Solutions
  249 N.Brand Boulevard # 316
  Glendale, CA 91203
  Tel. (800) 428-4229, 1 (818) 464-3582,
  Fax (818) 464-3770
  (covering California, Oregon, Washington, Arizona,
  Nevada, and Idaho)

  US East—The Aurora Group
  62 Leuning Street
  South Hackensack, NJ 07606
  Tel. 1 (800) 318-3934, Fax (201) 488-0058
  (covering Maine, New Hampshire, Vermont, Rhode Island,
  Massachusetts, Connecticut, New York, New Jersey,
  Pennsylvania, Delaware, Maryland, Virginia, West Virginia,
  and North Carolina)

US Southeast—Harmonix Corp.
141 NW 20th Street # H-1
Boca Raton, FL 33431
Tel. (561) 447-7170
Fax (561) 447-7133
(covering Florida, Georgia, South Carolina, Alabama, and
Tennessee)

Walker Tape
9620 Hawley Park Road
West Jordan, UT 84088
Tel. (801) 282-2015 or (800) 759-5150
Fax (801) 282-2131
E-mail: walkertape@aol.com

Wella
12 Mercedes Drive
Montvale, NJ 07645
(201) 930-1020
http://www.wella.com

Journals

Hair Loss Journal
American Hair Loss Council

*International Journal of Cosmetic Surgery and
Aesthetic Dermatology*
Editorial Board of Cross-Field Global Experts

Journal of the American Medical Association
American Medical Association

National Psoraisis Foundation Bulletin
National Psoraisis Foundation

Web Sites for Women's Hair Loss with Chat Forums and Support Pages

http://www.hairlosstalk.com
http://www.hairsite.com
http://www.hairtoday.com
http://www.hairtransplantnetwork.com
http://www.regrowth.com
http://www.rogaineforwomen.com
http://www.womenshairinstitute.com

Other Web Sites for Information on Doctors, Local Centers, Education, and to Learn About and Order Products

http://www.aaawigbiz.com
http://www.acewigs.com
http://www.ahlc.org
http://www.aimforherbs.com
http://www.beautifulhairagain.com
http://www.blackwomenrejoice.com
http://www.bosley.com
http://www.centerforimage.com
http://www.chemocareheadwear.com
http://www.cheryn.com (eyelashes/wigs)
http://www.chrissyv.com (cold-bond extension system)

http://www.colormebeautiful.com
http://www.cyberhair1.com
http://www.ethnicsoul.com
http://www.eyebrowz.com
http://www.farrellhair.com
http://www.follicle.com
http://www.hair-international.com
http://www.hairagain.com
http://www.hairgenesis.com
http://www.hairgrowthsolutions.com
http://www.hairloss-hair-loss.com
http://www.hairlossdirect.com
http://www.hairsupport.com
http://www.headcovers.com
http://www.hollycosmetics.com (prosthetics, cosmetics, wigs)
http://www.howstuffworks.com
http://www.inhousepharmacy.com
http://www.internationalhairgoods.com
http://www.isadesigns.com
http://www.ishrs.org
http://www.jacquelynwigs.com
http://www.keratin.com
http://www.ladiesofthelight.com (cancer and radiation hair loss)
http://www.menopause-metamorphosis.com
http://www.mhrw.com
http://www.micropointlink.com
http://www.minniepauz.com
http://www.natural-hair.com
http://www.notjustwigs.com
http://www.peggyknight.com (wigs/prosthetics)
http://www.plasticsurgery.org

http://www.regrow.com (Spencer Forrest)
http://www.revivogen.com
http://www.sheitel.com (Hana Wigs)
http://www.studiosf.com
http://www.thehatspot.com
http://www.thyroid-info.com
http://www.transgender.com
http://www.wigplus.com
http://www.women-thinning-hair-loss.com
http://www.worldofhair.com
http://www.worldofwigs.com

Books

Barrera, Alfonso, ed. *Hair Transplantation: The Art of Micrografting and Minigrafting* (with CD-ROM). St. Louis: Quality Medical Publications, 2001.

Bergfeld, Wilma, M.D. *A Woman Doctor's Guide To Skin Care.* Hyperion Books, New York: 1996.

Buchman, Dian Dincin. *The Complete Herbal Guide to Natural Health and Beauty.* New Canaan, CT: Keats Publishing, 1994.

Cheung, Theresa, and James W. Douglas. *Androgen Disorders in Women: The Most Neglected Hormone Problem.* Alaneda, CA: Hunter House, 1999.

Gewirtzman, Garry, M.D. *Skin Sense: A Dermatologist's Complete Guide to Your Family's Skin Care.* Hollywood, FL: Lifetime Books, Inc., 1993.

Golden, Manine Rosa. *Home Spa: Recipes and Techniques to Restore and Refresh.* New York: Abbeville Press, 1997.

Greenwood-Robinson, Maggie. *Hair Savers For Women: A Complete Guide to Preventing and Treating Hair Loss*. New York: Three Rivers Press, 2000.

Hitzig, Gary S., M.D. *Help and Hope For Hair Loss*. New York: Avon Press, 2000.

Kingsley, Philip. *Hair: An Owner's Handbook*. London: Aurum Press Limited, 1995.

Kobren, Spencer David. *The Bald Truth*. New York: Pocket Books, 1998.

Kobren, Spencer David. *The Truth About Women's Hair Loss*. New York: McGraw-Hill, 2000.

Mancuso, Kevin. *The Mane Thing*. Boston: Little, Brown and Co., 1999.

Sadick, Neil S. *Your Hair, Helping to Keep It: Treatment and Prevention of Hair Loss for Men and Women*. Yonkers, NY: Donald Richardson, Consumer Reports Books, 1991.

Steel, Elizabeth. *The Hair Loss Cure: How to Treat Alopecia and Thinning Hair*. Willing Borough, UK: Thorsons Publishing.

Thompson, Wendy, Jerry Shapiro, and Vera H. Price. *Alopecia Areata: Understanding and Coping With Hair Loss*. Baltimore: Johns Hopkins University Print, 2000.

Turkington, Carol A., and Jeffrey S. Dover, M.D. *Skin Deep: An A-Z of Skin Disorders, Treatments and Health*. New York: Facts on File, Inc., 1998.

Trade Publications

American Salon
270 Madison Avenue
New York, NY 10016
(212) 951-6600

Hair and Beauty News
302 The Cezanne
712 West 48th Street
Kansas City, MO 64112
(876) 756-3336

Hair International News
124-B East Main Street
P.O. Box 273
Palmyra, PA 17078
(717) 838-0795

Modern Salon
370 Lexington Avenue
Suite 2001
New York, NY 10017
(212) 682-7777

Salon News
Fairchild Publications
7 West 34th Street
New York, NY 10001
(212) 630-3547

SalonOvations
P.O. Box 98
El Paso, IL 61738
(309) 527-5060

INDEX

International Food Information
        Council, 96
International Hair Goods, 50, 59,
        119, 147, 176, 199
Invisible Hair, 148–149, 155
Involutional alopecia, 16
Iron deficiency, 95
Ironing products, 80
Isa Designs, 215–216

J

Jayne, Charlotte, 50, 57–58
Jeffrey Paul Institute, xiv–xv

K

Keratin, 97
Kerchiefs, with hair additions, 215
Kinky hair, 6
Knight, Robin, 119

L

Laser comb, 105
Laser Hair Care, 104–105
Laser therapy, 68, 97, 103–106
    cost of, 103–104, 228
    for men vs. women, 228
    side effects of, 105
Laser transplants, 226–229
    and donor hair, 228
    and hair loss, continued, 229
    and risk factor, 226–228

Leavitt, Matt, xiv, 14, 18,
        222–226, 227, 229, 231,
        232
Lefkowitz, Isa, 215–217
Lichen plano pilaris, 109
Lifestyle, of client, 41, 42–43
Lifting products, 80–81
Lineal extensions, 116–118
    application of, 131, 133,
        136–137
    cost of, 131, 138–139
    and evaluation, 134
    and measurement, 135
    profile, 132–133
    removal of, 137
    step-by-step instructions,
        134–136
    and strand-by-strand extensions,
        combining of, 139
    tool list, 133–134
    See also Extensions
Love International, 220
Lupus erythematosus, and alopecia,
        15, 109, 214

M

Machine-made integrations, 146
Machine-made wefts, 117
Machine-made wigs, 192
Madonna, 2, 219
Maintenance, of replacement hair.
        *See under individual hair
        replacement options*
Mancuso, Kevin, 5, 6
The Mane Thing (Mancuso), 5

cost of, 50, 52, 60–61
designs, 62–63
kinds of, 47. *See also* Human
    replacement hair; Natural
    replacement hair; Synthetic
    (man–made) replacement
    hair
preparation of, 54–60
quality of, 60–61
Reshapers, 16
Restoring Beautiful Hair Program, xv
Retail station
    and physical layout and
        equipment, for hair restoration
        business, 248
Rheumatoid arthritis, and alopecia
    areata, 15
Ribbon wefts, 118, 148
Riggs, Paul, 227–229, 234
Risk factor. *See under individual
    hair replacement options*
Rogaine, 104
    side effects of, 106–107
Rollabout cart, as equipment for hair
    restoration business, 243
Ross, Gary, 97

S

Salon professionals, xv–xvi. *See
    also* Cosmetic therapists
Salon-spa business. *See* Hair
    restoration business
Sassoon, Vidal, xiii
Saw palmetto, 97, 112

Scalp
    condition of, 14
    massage, 111
    and skin conditioners, 84
Scalp lifting, 232–233
    for men vs. women, 233
    and risk factor, 233
    vs. hair transplant, 230–231
Scalp reduction, 230–232
    and African-American women,
        231–232
    and hair loss, continued, 230
    for men vs. women, 230, 231
    and risk factor, 230, 231–232
    and scarring, 230, 232
    vs. hair transplant, 230–231,
        232
Scarring, and scalp reduction, 230,
    232
Scarves
    as hair alternative, 213, 215
    silk, and extensions, 142–143
Scott, Susan Craig, 17–18
Scruncis, with hair additions,
    218
Seborrhea, 26
Security issues, 176, 190, 199,
    216
Self-confidence, and hair loss, xii
Self-esteem, and hair loss, xii, 2
Semi-custom hair replacement,
    62–63
Semi-custom wigs, 192
Sexual dysfunction, and hair loss
    treatment, 27
Sexuality, and hair loss, xi